Diary of a Ghost Whisperer

Laura Powers

Hi Lindsey,
Thanks so much for your support & for working with the light!
much love to you,
Laura Powers

Copyright © 2015 Laura Powers

Cover Photo by Penny O Photography

All rights reserved. This book may not be reproduced in whole or in part, or transmitted in any form, without the written permission from the publisher except by a reviewer who may quote brief passages in review.

Library of Congress Data Available Upon Request

ISBN 978-0-9883026-7-9

First Printing, April 2015

Dedication

This book is dedicated to all the souls who have had traumatic lives and deaths and are seeking the light. It is my hope that through education, more people can understand their plight and receive training to help them cross and stop their suffering.

Acknowledgements

I'd like to recognize all those who helped me on my journey and assisted with the creation of this book. This includes the many teachers and educators who assisted me and paved the path for this information to be shared. There is a huge renaissance happening in the world right now regarding spirituality; I wouldn't be able to do the work I do now without the efforts of others before me to illuminate the often misunderstood world of spirit. In particular, I acknowledge Joan of Arc for standing strong with her convictions. I'd also like to recognize all of the women who were burned as witches during the Salem witch trials and during the inquisitions. Sadly women who had gifts like mine were accused of devil craft, Satanism or worse. I also appreciate all the teachers, living and in spirit form, who have taught me. Lastly, I recognize all of the spirit guides and angels who help me with my life and work – I couldn't be here without the constant support, education and guidance I receive from them and my spirit council.

Special Thanks

A big thank you to all those who helped with the creation of this book! Of course, I want to thank my angels and spirit guides as well as the living contributors. A profound thank you to my mother, Christine, who is an incredible inspiration to me, as well as a great supporter. Thank you also to all my clients for supporting my work in this field and for seeing the possibility in making changes through spirituality and energy-work. A big round of thanks to all who helped fund the book and preordered copies! Thank you to Sara and Sean O'Keefe for being great friends and being with me through the tough times and the good times. Thank you to my cousins, Laura and Laura, I am so glad we are so close and I am thankful for your help with my work and for being in my life! To Jan, thanks for helping and supporting me as I got started on this journey. To Rex, thank you for helping me learn and grow in ways I couldn't even have imagined! And thank you to my good friend Alesa for being with me on this wild ride. Sending love and appreciation to all of you who are reading this – you are truly loved and supported by the angels!

A special thank you so all those who contributed and pre-ordered copies of this book, without you, this book wouldn't have been possible. Thank you to the following:

Andrew Novick, Andy Kay, Anne Starke, Anton Riehl, Brandi Smith, Carolyn Elliot, Carrie Cono Soto, Cherri Pruitt, Christine Webb, Christine Berg, Christopher Hancock, Chris Davis, Cindy Morris, Claudia Hall, Cyndi Langley, David Johnson, David Clarke, Elizabeth Granai, Erik Moore, Gonzalo Serrano, Jan Lund, Jim Mercado, John Corsa, Joseph Canaday, Judy Hartman, Kati Johnson, Ken DeBacker, Kristen Bair, Lynne Manchester, Maggie Shandoff, Mark Ogle, Michael Martinez, Michelle White, Morgan Dennis-Ogreen, Naomi Campbell, Paul Karantonis, Penny Tharp, Rebecca Abraxas, Renee Pichette, Richard Fabian, Sidney Stoper, Stacy LeDoux, Susan Wei, Terri Runnings

Table of Contents

Introduction

This book is a book that has been many years in the making. I have learned so much through my work as a psychic medium, ghost whisperer, and from a lifetime of seeing and sensing the spiritual realm. I wanted to share some of the most interesting stories from my work for a variety of reasons. Some of them are wild and sometimes hard to believe. Some provide insight into the spiritual world and some are quite touching.

I recommend reading chapters one and two on how I got into this work, and after that you can read it from front to back or you can jump around and read it by chapter. If you'd like to know more about my history and how I got into this very interesting line of work, you can read my first book, *Life and the After Life: Notes from a Medium and Angel Communicator*. If you want to learn more about angels and how to connect with them, you can read my second book, *Angels: How to Understand, Recognize, and Receive their Guidance*.

I find that lots of people are interested in ghosts and things that are scary. I do tell some tales of scary ghosts but my aim is to help people understand this realm and shed some light on the often misunderstood world of ghosts and spirits. Sometimes things are scary just because we don't understand them. In this realm, knowledge is truly power, and just by reading this book, you will learn a lot of helpful information too. Happy reading!

ONE
What I Do

You know when you are at a party or on a plane and someone asks what you do? When asked that question, I tend to answer that I am a psychic medium, or a ghost whisperer and, boy, do I get a lot of unusual responses! I've had people laugh out loud (I think they thought I was joking), get really quiet and then excuse themselves, or want to ask me about a bazillion questions. I haven't seen any statistics, but being a psychic has to be one of the most unusual professions in the world. Very often when I tell people what I do, they tell me that they have never met someone who does this before. This is not unusual! If being a psychic is unusual, being a ghost whisperer is even more unusual. It's kind of like having a really unusual specialty in medicine; there aren't a lot of us doing this work. When I first got into this work I struggled to find teachers. There just weren't many people who did this and I needed help figuring out where to start. Luckily, I did eventually find teachers who helped me get started and then I did a lot of hands-on learning. One of my missions now is to get even more people trained in this profession because this type of work greatly improves the lives of those who are dealing with spirits and also helps earth bound spirits or ghosts cross over and be at peace.

Ghost Whispering

I do work most of the time as a psychic, but a growing part of my business is working as a ghost whisperer, paranormal communicator and demon clearer. I realize this scares a lot of people, but let me assure you that it doesn't have to be scary as long as you are prepared for what you are getting into and that you are receiving psychic protection. It is actually very fascinating work as no two clients and situations are the same. I also often get to see immediate and longer term shifts with clients which are nothing short of incredible! When I was younger, this realm terrified me, but now I love what I do.

In many ways, I function as a counselor for ghosts. I arrive, chat with whoever is there, find out why they have not transitioned into the light to the other side, and then help them cross. I might also deal with dark entities and demons and have them escorted away. For those who have been living with these beings in their home or business spaces, this is such a relief! For the ghosts who have been trapped here, it can end years, decades, or centuries of misery. In some cases, the living occupants have been downright tortured by these beings, or in other cases, they are simply not happy with the energy around them. In more extreme cases, my clients want to stop the enormous expenses that are resulting from problems and accidents caused by these beings. Wherever unhappy ghosts and dark entities are, dysfunction reigns and weird plumbing problems are the norm! If you have a money pit where everything keeps breaking, you very well could have some of these beings sharing your living space. Oftentimes, when there is a lot of dark entity and ghost activity in a space, it can also result in illness.

The stories told here are some of the more extreme ones, but many places have ghosts that are far less intense and noticeable. The truth is, we are sharing this earth with many beings that don't have physical bodies and many of them, like ghosts, would be better off if they crossed over. If you have ghosts in your home, know that the best thing for them is to cross over. The benefits to hiring a ghost whisperer to clear these beings and shift the space are innumerable! If you wonder if you have one of these beings in your space, it is highly likely that you do. Find a reputable ghost whisperer to help you! There are many who have trained with me or I can travel to you. I am currently accepting students who want to learn about this field. For more information, you can go to my website www.healingpowers.net. Bear in mind that sometimes this work can be done remotely too. There is no distance in the energy world, so work in this realm can be done in person or remotely.

I hope you enjoy these stories from my work and that they provide insight into this often misunderstood spiritual realm.

TWO
How I Got to be a Ghost Whisperer

I was a very psychic child. If you had asked me about that as a girl, I probably wouldn't have known what you were talking about, but I would have denied it even if I had understood. If I had been honest, I probably would have told you I was crazy, since no one else seemed to sense and see what I did. To make matters worse, a lot of the things I saw were at night or with my mind's eye or third eye which made me think maybe I was making it all up. This made for a tough childhood, adolescence and young adulthood as I was constantly attacked and beset by dark energy beings that terrified me. I was scared to tell my parents or anyone because I didn't want to be labeled as crazy. Plus, I was pretty sure there wasn't anything that any of the adults in my life could do about it. As I got older, my abilities got stronger and more intense and so did the visitations. Spirits tried to get in my body and dark entities fed on my fear. I was terrified. By the way, if you have a sensitive child, please do not assume that they will tell you if anything like this is going on. I didn't tell my mom about anything I saw until I was in college. She was shocked, though later she said that in retrospect, a lot more things about me made sense.

What triggered this sudden shift and opening for me was that a family friend described a ghost that was on my parents' property. There was an older male ghost who was quite territorial and had been terrorizing me for quite some time. He enjoyed watching me while I slept and I would awake to see him standing at the foot of the bed in the middle of the night. He invaded my mind and my dreams and wanted to me to drink liquor so he could occupy my body to experience drinking through me. He tried to convince me that I should let him possess me for a little while. He seemed to hate me and women, in general. He broke things in my home and would change the channel on the television or the radio, usually turning the channel to something scary or scary sounding like the movie *The Dead* or *The Killing Room.* He made me feel unsafe and unwelcome in my own home. Once he appeared so real to me that I almost called the cops when, from the backyard, I watched a man walk up the stairs to the entryway to the guest house I was staying in. I thought he was a live person until he got to the door and fuzzed out and went through the door.

I was terrified of him and also terrified of myself, fearful that I was really and truly insane. Then one day a family friend came to get some of his belongings from the garage. He went into the garage and came out white-faced and shaken. I asked what was wrong and he gave a detailed description of the ghost that I'd been struggling with. This changed my life because I finally had confirmation from another person that at least some of what I sensed was not the creation of my imagination. I realized this ghost could not be created by my delusional mind since someone else had seen him. I had never spoken a word to anyone about him. I was both thrilled and even more terrified. On the one hand

I was not crazy, but on the other hand this ghost was real and I had no idea how to handle the situation, which made me even more frightened. I did the only thing I knew to do. I tried to shut down my psychic gifts. As far as I could tell, they were only causing me problems.

I am a very determined person, so once I decide to do something; it is very hard to dissuade me from doing it. I shut everything out: what I heard, what I saw, and even what I felt around me, though that was harder. If you have ever seen the movie *Constantine* with Keanu Reeves, there is a situation in the movie which illustrates exactly what I did. In the movie, Keanu's character plays a demon-slayer of sorts. There is a lead female character, a human who once had a twin. As girls, she and her sister both saw demons and other creatures. The other twin told her parents what they were seeing. Concerned, the parents took them both to see a psychiatrist. When asked, the other twin told the truth about seeing demons, but her sister lied and said she saw nothing. As they got older, the other twin was put in an insane asylum and eventually committed suicide, while her sister led a relatively normal life and eventually stopped seeing the beings that she had told others she couldn't see. The mind is very powerful and whatever we suggest to be true will start to create our reality. If you do this lovingly and positively, you can create and manifest amazing things. You can learn more about this in my forthcoming book about manifesting, *Angels & Manifesting*. However, if you are living in fear and denial, you will manifest more fear and situations that require denial.

I chose the latter path at that time. In my defense, I really didn't know what else to do. I'd tried to read a few books about ghosts, but none of them really seemed to do much to help me. My parents had no experience and suggested I be strong, which helped to a degree but still left me feeling lost. This was before a lot of shows like *Medium* and *Ghost Whisperer* made this topic more mainstream. Prior to this I really did feel pretty much like a freak and was trying to conform to the normal. So I shut down. Like the character in *Constantine*, I shut out what I saw and eventually stopped seeing them.

The problem with this approach was that everything I had seen or sensed was still there. Much like an ostrich sticking its head in the sand, I could no longer see these beings, but they were still there and they were still seeing me. On the positive side, I was not afraid since I couldn't see them, but these beings have power and the ability to do things to us. They can feed on our energy like parasites and affect our mood and wellbeing. All of this was still happening to me even though I was trying to shut it out. Just because I wasn't seeing them anymore, didn't mean that these beings weren't still having an impact. It took many years for me to understand the negative consequences of shutting down like I did.

Fast forward several years and I was living what I thought was a successful life, doing all the things that you are supposed to do to be deemed "successful" in our society. I had a successful and notable career in higher education, had mostly completed my master's degree, had run for office and was on several boards and public committees, performed in local theaters in my spare time, was married, and had a nice new home. Everything seemed perfect until all of a sudden it really, really wasn't. The house of cards came tumbling down until the life I'd spent years carefully constructing was in ruins around me. I became unemployed right at the start of the recession, I was physically ill with several diagnoses including depression, and PCOS (poly-cystic ovary syndrome), I was 40 pounds overweight, and I was on sleeping pills. The straw that broke the camel's back came when I learned that my husband (who I had known since I was 14), was having a devastating affair with a very young woman. I even learned that they had been shopping for wedding dresses as if he and I weren't still together. I had recently left my career, family, and home in Colorado to move to Seattle with him for his career. I was in a new city, with no job, in the worst economy of my lifetime. I felt betrayed and trapped. Every aspect of my life was in ruins.

I was desperate and felt alone. I thought I had done everything right, so how had I gotten to this miserable place? On a visit to my hometown while trying to figure out what to do and how to put my life back together, I went to a psychic. What she told me shocked me but ultimately was just what I needed to hear to turn my life around. She talked about how I had shut out my intuition and my psychic abilities and how I had shut out the good with the bad. I had also shut out what I needed to know. My husband, who had seemed like a saint, had proved to be a wolf in sheep's clothing. My husband and I went to counseling and the counselor did not allow me to blame my husband for everything. He too suggested that there must have been signs, that I must have known on some level that something was wrong. I wanted so desperately to blame my husband for all my problems, but I knew that wasn't productive and it wasn't true. I was forced to look into the mirror and ask myself how I had let myself get into this awful situation. I then set the intention to open my intuition back up, take classes and learn how to use my gifts, mostly so that I would never, ever get into that situation again.

I started to take classes, and read voraciously on the topics of spirits, ghosts, angels and even quantum physics. I was reading a book every week or sometimes every couple of days. I started connecting with the light forces and not just the dark, and slowly but surely my life began to change. I had an incredible angelic

experience after I invited the light and angels into my l'
from there on, I knew I was not alone. Since I had set the
to open back up, it was as if the floodgates opened and I was inundated with the energy and visions of ghosts and other beings that I had been shutting out for years. Though I felt stronger, I needed help dealing with all of this. I hired two teachers to help me learn how to communicate with ghosts safely and effectively and how to help them cross to the other side.

This was extremely helpful, as earth-bound spirits or ghosts are attracted to those who can see and sense them, even if that person doesn't know what to do! It was as if these ghosts could tell that I could help them even before I knew that I could. It is very much like the movie *Ghost Town*, where the main character dies for a short time while under anesthesia and comes back seeing ghosts. They could see me and I could see and sense them and they flooded into my life. I would have several ghosts in my room while I was trying to sleep (it was hard to rest)! I would even have ghosts follow me home on the plane from other states. Thank goodness I was able to find teachers that helped me learn how to safely open up the light, transition the ghosts to the other side and clear the space energetically. I also took classes to develop my psychic gifts, at first for my personal development and as a hobby.

The more work and training I received in this realm, the more it became clear that this was really my calling. Initially, I was very resistant to this work. I had my master's degree in Political Science, I was used to dealing with everything very logically, and had never envisioned myself working as a psychic – the very idea seemed to go against everything I had ever been taught to believe or think. Then again look where that got me! Gradually, I opened up to the concept and started giving readings, doing energy healing, and helping others who had ghost or demon activity in their homes or businesses. Once I entered this field, things changed for me very quickly. I had to do a lot of personal work releasing fear, beliefs and patterns I had about doing this work. Gradually the work paid off and I was able to enjoy my new career, making a living doing something that utilized my natural gifts and helped others (both the living and the dead). What had previously felt like a curse, became a blessing.

Ghosts don't necessarily respect that I am "off the clock" so to speak, so I have helped a lot of spirits cross over in my personal time as well. The ghost that used to watch me sleep found peace and transitioned to the after-life. Thankfully, he is now on the other side and not trapped here trying to find a way to release his anger and feed his addiction. The stories in this book are some of the more interesting examples of ghosts and spirit interactions that I have come across in my life so far. There are some celebrities, some sweet ghosts, some that are angry, and some that made me afraid. Each spirit I have come across has taught me something new and I am grateful to be able to share their stories with you.

Since everyone who does this work is different, I'll share with you a little bit about how I receive information. I am clairvoyant which means clear-seeing. I do sometimes see within the physical realm but most of the time, I close my eyes so I can see more clearly in the spirit realm without the physical getting in the way. I am also clairaudient which means clear-hearing and for me that usually manifests as hearing words or phrases. Occasionally these words or phrases are heard as whispers or spoken words but most of the time it is like they are beamed into my head and I hear the words in my mind, very much like telepathy. I am also very empathic and clairsentient, which means clear-feeling. I feel other people's energy and emotions in my body. I also can tune in and get a read in advance about certain outcomes using this gift. Lastly, I am also clair-cognizant which means clear-knowing. Sometimes I know things without knowing why. When I do my work, I use all of these psychic senses to get information. The spirit realm is often more subtle than the physical realm, so when I see things, they are often more fuzzy or less clear than things seen here on the physical plane. You can read more about these and other helpful terms used in this book in the helpful terms section. You can also look at the recommended reading list and sources for additional information on related topics.

THREE
What is a Ghost Really? What Else is There?

Some people are very frightened of ghosts and even the idea that they are real can strike terror in the hearts of some otherwise very tough people! I hope to alleviate your fear about them through this book by giving you an understanding of what they are and what they aren't.

As live beings, we all have a spirit and a body. Most people recognize this dual aspect. When our body dies, the spirit separates from it. This can also happen during out-of-body experiences (OBEs) which can include near-death experiences (NDEs) and astral travel, which simply means travelling in the astral or non-physical planes during sleep or meditation.

When we die and cross over, the energetic connections between our body and our soul are completely severed. If we are having some kind of out-of-body experience, the soul remains energetically connected to the physical body. When someone dies, the light opens up which acts as a gateway or portal to the other side. After a period of time, the light goes away and the gate closes too. If the spirit of the one whose body has died has not crossed over into the light by then, the soul is trapped here on the physical plane. At that time, they become a ghost or earth-bound spirit. Basically, they are a person without a body.

A spirit who has crossed into the light has a very different perspective from one who hasn't. A spirit in the light goes through a life review process that gives them a broader perspective and a bigger understanding of their life and why things happened the way they did. Spirits in the light are also free to come back and forth at will. They are, generally speaking, at peace and enjoying their experience on the other side. They tend to be less hung-up on things that happened or didn't happen here on earth.

Ghosts, on the other hand, have not gotten the life-review and tend to be scared, angry, or sad and simply are not letting go of the old. There are some ghosts who just want to hang out and are in a relatively peaceful mental state but that is rare. Even if a ghost is not angry or upset, the best thing for that spirit really is to cross over into the light. If they are not moving forward, they are stopping their progress and they are not feeling the peace that they would feel from crossing over. Imagine if you graduated from high school but instead of moving forward to college or getting a job, you simply kept going to high school indefinitely. There would be nothing more for you to gain from staying. So it is with ghosts. One thing I always tell earth bound spirits is that if they cross over and want to come back to wherever or whoever it is that they are haunting, they are welcome to do so. But they almost never do because once they cross, they realize all the other experiences they can have at their disposal. They still can and very frequently do visit family if their family members are still alive.

Bear in mind that time does not necessarily pass the same way for ghosts as it does for those who are alive. When I first ved back to my hometown, Lafayette, Colorado, after psychically opening back up, I was completely overwhelmed with the number of very old ghosts. By old, I mean that the ghosts had been around for a very long time, in some cases for over one-hundred years. Lafayette is a mining town and is, therefore relatively old for a city in Colorado. Also, mining towns tend to create a lot of ghosts. When the teacher I brought in to help train me communicated with the ghosts in my home in Old Town Lafayette, I was amazed at how many of them were bringing up old wounds and hurts and were very angry at people who had wronged them over 100 years prior! They were very angry about it as if those things had just happened to them because I am sure to them it seemed that way. In fact, some ghosts keep reliving or redoing the same thing over and over again. This would be similar to someone with amnesia living the same day again and again, not understanding what was happening.

This lack of understanding can also make some ghosts very disoriented or confused about what is happening. They might be angry or frustrated at why you are in their home! For a good depiction of this, I recommend seeing the movie *The Others* with Nicole Kidman. It portrays that very well. Some ghosts do not realize they are dead, and as a result, they have a very skewed vision of what is actually happening.

There are some ghosts that do understand they are dead and still choose to be here. For some ghosts this is because they like it here, or they want to stay in their home or city. Sometimes however, ghosts know they are dead and they enjoy the rise they can get out of people by making them afraid. They feed on the terror and fear that they bring out in people through their actions.

What a Ghost is Not

A ghost is not a demon, an angel, a spirit guide, an entity, or a faerie. All of these other beings are real, but they are quite different in nature. Remember a ghost is simply a person without a body on the earth plane. Because they are in essence a disincarnated person who is trapped here, they still have free will. This means that neither you, nor I, or even an angel can force a ghost to do anything. However, we can enforce our own boundaries and work with the angels for this purpose. This is where I and other ghost whisperers come in. Basically, we can work with the angels to help counsel the ghosts and help them understand why crossing over is a good idea and then assist them in doing that. In other words, I work as a ghost counselor! If you do have a ghost that is giving you troubles, I highly recommend that you ask Archangel Michael and the angels to help protect you and escort the ghost away from you. The angels act as our spiritual bouncers and protectors. This can be tricky if the ghost or ghosts feel that they belong in the space (for example if they lived there prior to you), because in a way their ownership precedes yours. In cases like this, the only way to get them to really leave you alone is to help them cross. So for example, if you moved into a home but the previous tenant was there still and both of you felt you had a right to be there, it would get complicated so bringing in outside resources like angels and ghost whisperers can help.

Sometimes people get confused about which type of energy being they are dealing with and assume, sometimes inaccurately, that they are dealing with a ghost. Below is a short description of some other beings that might be interacting with you.

Angels

An angel is an energy being that is a mediator between the creator and us. The word "angel" comes from the Greek word for messenger, because one of their primary functions is to take our prayers to and from heaven. Though they are not angels, oftentimes our loved ones in heaven can act like angels for us, by watching over us. An angel is inherently different than a human, though even this can be a gray area as there are angels that have chosen to incarnate in human form. For more information on this, you can read the book *Earth Angels* by Doreen Virtue.

Angels are divine beings of light who are here to help us in our work and in our life path. They will only ever help and never harm. They give us loving, gentle guidance and assistance, though they honor our free will and do need our permission to intervene on our behalf. One exception to this rule is if we are going to die before our time. In these cases, they do intervene, often resulting in profound miracles. They are constantly communicating with us, trying to help us do whatever is the best for us. Most of us do not receive their messages because we don't understand how these messages come through. For more details on that process, you can read my book *Angels: How to Understand, Recognize, and Receive Their Guidance.*

Demons

Just as an angel is a being of the light who is here to helps us, demons are beings of the dark who are here with the opposite intent. Angels are creative and light and demons are dark and destructive. Angels are beings of pure love and demons feed on fear, hate, anger, frustration, and related emotions. Angels are cooperative and demons are about opposition. Think yin and yang

and you will start to get a sense of their differences. D
always want something whereas angels help because t
loving and want to do so. I do not understand those th
deals or agreements with demons (yes this does happen) because the angels will help you with no strings attached. There is no catch with angels but you can never, ever, trust a demon. I do not recommend communicating or engaging with them.

Most people are on the middle path in life, which means they have experienced both light and dark forces in their life. One of the main differences between how the light and the dark operate is that the light honors our free will and waits to intervene until we ask. The dark is not so polite and will come into your life without your permission. You must actively choose the light and say 'no' to the dark, if you want a life filled with love, light and joy. The analogy I give clients is that our mind, our lives and our energy fields are very much like a garden. If you don't want weeds in your garden you have to remove them, and conversely, flowers must be planted. Angels are like flowers and demons (and ghosts) are like weeds. Unless you actively choose the light and then take actions to support that decision, the dark will be there by default.

To be clear, ghosts are not demons, but they are also not of the light since they chose not to go into it when their body passed. This means that, often times, their motivations are not loving. Also, since demons feed on fear, anger, hate, resentment, sadness, etc. (and many ghosts are in those emotional states), demons can continue to feed on their energy and emotions just like they do on those who are living. This means that where you find ghosts, you will also often find demons and vice versa.

Both a ghost and a demon can possess you, though the extreme cases of possession that we tend to hear about are demon possession. Generally speaking demons are more powerful than ghosts though ghosts can learn to siphon off energy from living beings and then use that energy. The ones that have learned to do that tend to be the angriest and most challenging ghosts to deal with.

The clearing process for demons and dark entities (to be discussed a bit later) is completely different than for ghosts. A ghost still has free will since they are a person simply without a body. A demon does not have the same rights here. You can ask the angels to remove demons and they will help. If the demon is very powerful, you may raise your vibration and get yourself further in the light so that the beings of the dark cannot reach you. Those that get the most attacked by dark entities and demons are sometimes starting on the light path but still accessible by the dark. The farther you go into the light, the harder it is for the dark beings to reach you. As Winston Churchill once said, "If you are going through hell, keep going." In other words, if you are in the light path where they can still reach you, don't stop, keep going into the light!

Additionally, those that mess with dark forces, black magic, Ouija boards, etc. risk inviting these energy and dark beings in their life.

Dark Entities

A dark entity is a being that is not of the light, and that does not belong here on the earth plane. They, like demons, feed on dark energy like fear, pain, sadness, etc. I believe they do not belong here because when I ask the angels to remove them, they do so whereas with ghosts, I have to reason with the ghost and get them to figure out why this is a good idea. I believe that dark entities are from a different plane or place and that they use earth as their feeding and playing ground. Some of the types that are commonly seen look like the following and feed on the following things:

- Spiders – feed on and create fear
- Snakes – feed on and create pain
- Trilobite (a type of prehistoric marine animal that looks like a large insect often found in the fossil record) - feed on and create sadness and hopelessness
- Gremlins – feed on and create depression, malaise and isolation
- Flies – feed on and create dissension, miscommunication and hopelessness.

Some of these beings may also be classified as minor demons, or beings from another plane. The entities that have a humanoid fly appearance (very much like Jeff Goldblum's appearance in the movie *The Fly*) are very intelligent and manipulative. Please note that these are not the same thing as animal totems or spirits. One of my spirit guides is a spider and that is a helpful spirit, whereas a spider entity is not there for your good and, in fact, feeds on dark energy. In the future, I will be writing another book on entities and demons and how they operate. If you suspect one of these beings is around, you can always book a reading or a clearing session. At the minimum, I strongly recommend calling on Archangel Michael and asking him to remove any beings that are not of the light and take them PERMANENTLY away from you. This permanent part is important. When I started doing the entity removals, I was largely self-taught and if I didn't ask for them to be permanently removed, they would just come back. Also ask the angels to remove any energy or attachments that these beings have left behind.

These dark entities can be stubborn. Keep asking the angels for help with this until you feel better and have faith that what you believe can happen. We are constantly manifesting and if we do not believe that they can be removed and if we are fearful, then that energy will win and the beings will remain there.

Poltergeists

Poltergeist activity is commonly characterized by moving objects, destruction and loud noises. Some believe that Poltergeists are angry ghosts while others believe they are a more malevolent entity. One potential explanation is that a poltergeist is a ghost who has demons attached and influencing him or her and thereby giving them increased power. I personally haven't experienced anything that I would classify as poltergeist activity so I can't speak from direct experience about them. They are a relatively rare supernatural phenomenon.

Faeries

Faeries are energy beings that, like humans, have egos. Faeries act like guardian angels for the plant and animal kingdom. Faeries can be loving, though they can also be mischievous. They tend to only show themselves to those they trust and those that are kind guardians and stewards to the plant and animal realm. Legend has it that they used to share the physical plane with us but that humans hunted and disrespected them and so they found a way to hide. If they show themselves to you, consider it an honor! Most of the faeries I have seen look very much like Tinkerbell is depicted in Peter Pan; like a ball of light with a human-like figure in the middle. They are quite enchanting and charming! If you'd like the faeries to reveal themselves to you, ask them to do so. You can also ask for the faeries to help with tasks that help animals or the earth.

These are just a sampling of the supernatural beings that interact with humans on earth. If you'd like to learn more about some of these other beings, stay tuned for more books on these topics. You can always go to www.healingpowers.net and subscribe to be notified about upcoming books and articles on these topics.

So now for some real ghost stories! If you get spooked while reading, ask Archangel Michael (he is a protector and leader of the armies of angels) and the angels to take away your fear and protect you. In fact, I encourage you to do that right now!

FOUR
The Ghost in the Closet

The stereotype of a ghost is one that is angry or sad and is destructive and angry towards those in the space the ghost also occupies. The story I will tell you next is about a ghost who was just the opposite. I was asked to do a clearing at a historic home after a mother with two kids moved in. She wanted to refresh the energy but, in addition to that, there had been a few unexplained things that had happened. Nothing was concerning, but the activity was making it hard for the mother to sleep due to the lights in her master bedroom closet turning on by themselves in the middle of the night.

Another strange occurrence had happened as the family was moving in. The movers had stacked the boxes in the basement to leave space in the rest of the house while it was being remodeled. After unloading, the movers came downstairs and sitting on top of one of the boxes was the drawing of a woman. No one seemed to know where it came from. It was set seemingly purposefully on top of the boxes and the room had previously been empty. No one aside from the movers and the family members had been there. No one could explain the presence of the picture or how it got there.

The mother of the family wanted to understand who or what was turning on the lights in her closet every night awakening her. She didn't feel there was anything bad there but she did want to understand and make sure that she and her children were safe. When I toured the house, I cleared some of the old energy that had been kicked up from the basement during the move. I cleared a few dark entities that feed on negative or stagnant energy much like a parasite. When I got to the master bedroom and went into the closet I was somewhat surprised to find the spirit of a woman in there. She was a little shy but had sweet energy. The client's closet was beautiful with newly constructed shelves, a lovely chandelier and beautiful clothes. It was a closet that many women could only dream about! The spirit of this woman was quite delighted to be in the beautiful closet and she showed me how she enjoyed spending time there. She would look in the mirror at herself and envision herself in all the beautiful clothes, relishing in the decadence of it. It was very sweet really! Here was a woman who had access to something she had never dreamed of in real- life and she loved it. This was simply a woman (without a body) enjoying her current situation! She also expressed to me that she really liked the family that she was staying with. She was in all ways very sweet!

After relaying this information to the client, I spoke with spirit for a short time, and explained that she could have any clothes and an even more fabulous closet on the other side. This is true! Once on the other side, you can have just about anything that you can envision. I also explained that once she crossed into the light she could still come back and visit, should she want to. Some ghosts will indeed choose to do this once they go into the light! Others get over to heaven or the other side and love it so much that they only leave to come here to visit and check in on family members. She was a little timid, but once I opened up the light and asked the angels to help her cross, she moved into it. The light acts like a gateway or a portal to the other side. She crossed into the light quickly and easily and the room felt calm and peaceful after she left. I contacted the client after the house blessing and the lights no longer turned themselves on in the closet. I do believe that she brought the picture with her and set it on top of the boxes as a way to say hello to the new family moving in.

She is, to this day, one of the sweetest ghosts that I have met and I cannot say that I blame her for haunting the beautiful closet!

FIVE
The Angriest Ghost I Have Ever Met

While some ghosts are sweet, like the one in the previous story, many of them are angry, sad, frustrated, or all of the above. These are the ghosts that really make their presence known. If one of these very angry ghosts is around, you are not likely to be able to ignore it. These are the ghosts that spooky movies are made about. I was invited to a large ranch with several buildings to help with several ghosts, including one in particular who was terrorizing the daughter of those who ran the ranch. The ghost threatened her while she was sleeping; he would stand at the foot of the bed, and was quite angry and intimidating. The daughter was very scared and quite psychic, which meant that she could see and hear this male ghost quite clearly.

I arrived at the ranch in the late afternoon and did some clearing of some dark entities in some other parts of the house before making my way to the bedroom where the daughter slept. By this time, it was near nightfall. One thing about this work is that it is tougher to do at night. The day is our time, the time for those who are of the light and the living. The night is the time when things that go bump in the night are stronger. To do this work safely and effectively, it is best to do clearing work during the day. Conversely, when I work in paranormal investigation, we do most of our work at night since that is when ghost activity is the strongest.

Since it was dusk, I received a clear message from the angels that it was not optimal to start with this particular spirit until daylight. I was also shown that the young woman's grandfather was trying to protect her from his influence. The angels suggested asking for their protection through the night and starting the work in the morning. The household, including myself, ate dinner and went to bed. I was sleeping in the room adjacent to the bedroom where this ghost was spending the most time. Throughout the night, I heard loud knocking sounds and though I was able to sleep and woke up rested, I knew there was a lot of activity.

At breakfast, I enquired about how everyone's night had gone, and unfortunately the daughter confirmed that she had not slept well. In fact, she had a dream in which the ghost in question had threatened that very bad things would happen to me and the family if they continued to have me there doing my work. I reassured her that this was not the case and that the ghost was just trying to do whatever he could to stop me from my work. Ghosts will say things like this because ghosts are scared of the unknown and that includes crossing over. It was also confirmed that no live occupant of the house had knocked on my door or wall the previous night so I knew it was the spirits. The daughter remained very frightened and left for the day, which was fine. She was truly scared about what this ghost would do if I continued my work!

Into her bedroom we went and it was immediately intense. I was glad I had not tried to tackle this situation after a long day. I needed all my energy to handle this particular ghost. My friend Jan and I had gone to this clearing together. She and I had been close ever since we worked together in the Office of the President at the University of Colorado. She and I became very close friends and bonded through intense and stressful times when the university administration was going through lots of turbulence and transition. When I went through my life transformation after my divorce and career shift, we realized we both had a great interest in exploring the unseen and unknown spiritual realm. She totally supported and assisted me in opening up to my gifts and was an amazing listener who helped me figure out this new spiritual world I was opening myself to. If you are opening yourself up psychically, I highly recommend surrounding yourself by those who are open-minded and supportive. We need all the help we can get when dealing with these realms, and having solid friends who support you is extremely instrumental in making the transition as smooth as possible. As an empath, I choose my friends very carefully since I am so sensitive to energy, and Jan is one of the good ones.

My friend Jan was operating the camera, (we were documenting our work for educational purposes), and as soon as we walked into the bedroom, we immediately became nauseous and light-headed. Even after asking the angels for protection, it was really challenging. This ghost was angry and hateful. He had been a ghost for several decades. He was psychically and energetically attacking me (sending hateful and targeted negative energy my way) and kept telling me that I wasn't going to get him to leave and that I was going to regret going there. I tried to communicate with him at that point, but he wouldn't listen.

After a short period of time, both Jan and I felt completely drained and we had to go outside to collect ourselves. Once outside, we asked the angels to clear the effects of the psychic attack; spirits can send you negative energy that coat your aura with negative slime, very much as depicted in the movie *Ghost Busters*. While I was being cleared, I asked the angels for guidance on how to help this particular ghost. What the angels showed me was that this man had led a very difficult life. He hadn't ever felt like he could get ahead. I was shown the image of this man being hammered into the ground like a nail. No one seemed to care for him and he led a bitter life. He died when a man stepped on his chest and slit his throat while he was sleeping. He awoke in a panic, in pain and choking on his own blood.

The chest constriction and nausea I felt in his presence was very much what he experienced at the time of his death. Since I am an empath, I often feel in my own body what the spirit is feeling. Because this man had felt so powerless in life, he lorded over his power in death. He loved making people scared and feeding on their fear because he had not had that experience of feeling any kind of power when he was alive. That said, he was still miserable and in a lot of fear and pain underneath that anger.

After the angels showed me this, I approached the ghost very differently. At first I had gone in with strong energetic shields and a lot of walls up. Even though I had good reason to approach him that way, I was defensive from the start. The next time I went inside, I immediately conveyed to the spirit that I had sympathy for what he had gone through. I said I was sorry that he'd had such a tough life and that I wished things had been easier. As soon as I started talking this time around, his energy towards me completely changed. He started crying and the feeling of anger shifted to a deep and incredible sadness and despair. I continued to describe to him that I couldn't change anything that had happened in his life, but that I could help him cross over. I also explained that once he crossed, he would no longer be trapped in the feeling of despair and he would be allowed to heal and experience joy. I was surprised at how quickly his energy had shifted from anger to sadness and realized that behind the anger was a lot of grief and also fear. This particular spirit was terrified. I spent some time consoling him and assuring him that everything would be okay.

He was starting to calm a bit, so I worked with the angels and opened up a portal of light to the other side. He was afraid, but I continued to talk with him and reassured him that all would be well. He was afraid that he would be punished for his sins (many ghosts are afraid of this), but I assured him that this wasn't how it worked. He would learn from what he did, and hopefully not repeat that pattern, but would be happy and at peace once he crossed over. Once the light was open, his mother came to greet him on the other side. She looked like Dorothy's Aunt Em in the *Wizard of Oz;* she was wearing a cotton dress and was slightly plump and very sweet. He moved towards her and into the light. She held out her arms and they embraced. I could feel the relief he experienced as he let go of all the worry, fear, and pain that he'd been holding onto for so long. I watched him retreat into the light and once he was completely through, I closed the portal to the other side.

I experienced great peace and a feeling of love with this particular experience. I learned a lot about human emotions. I learned that behind anger and aggression there is often simply sadness and fear. I learned to open my heart more. This particular spirit taught me a lot and I am so glad that I was able to help him and those who he'd been terrorizing. Fear can spread like a virulent disease. Those who are in fear can very easily spread fear to others around them. The opposite of fear is love. Many think that hatred and love are polar opposites but I believe that at the center of hatred is really fear and fear simply cannot be in the energy of love. Once I changed my energy and felt love and compassion for this man, his aggression dissolved and I could see that this was simply a sad, lost and broken man who desperately needed help. I believe that this is true with live people also. If we can be more loving, then we often can heal the hurt that is tearing people up inside. This is not the same thing as being a doormat. The importance is to balance helping with making sure that you are not being used or damaged in the process. If you are unsure how to do this, ask the angels for help finding a balanced way to help and be safe yourself.

SIX
Murder-suicide

There is one particular ghost clearing experience I will never forget because it was so sad and tragic. It involved both a murder and suicide, and even one person dying from either one of these causes can create an incredible amount of grief. Having one of each in a particular home can have a devastating impact on the energy of the home and make those living in the space feel sad and depressed. This was definitely the case at this particular home. Those who are very psychic will have a very hard time living with ghosts in this emotional situation. Imagine being around people that are murderous and depressed and you'll get an idea of what it might feel like.

I was called in to the house because of several ghosts on the premises but these two were some of the most intense. The man showed himself to me first – he had dark blond or light brown hair, was fit and very masculine. He was very angry and territorial. I asked for psychic protection from the angels but also immediately started asking him why he was so angry. He showed me a very tough childhood in which his father had beaten him since he's been small. It was so sad; he was a very sweet and sensitive tow-headed little boy. He was terrified because the beatings were so severe. I saw the brutality of what was aimed at him and felt that no child should be exposed to this kind of treatment. Because he was so small, he felt helpless in this situation. This left him angry and hurt and though he despised how he was treated, he learned the pattern of abuse and carried it on.

When he married his wife, things got worse. His anger grew over time and he kept all the rage for his father all bottled inside. He distrusted her and was jealous of her. He became convinced she was having an affair with someone he knew. He confronted her and she denied the affair, but he didn't believe her. In a fit of rage, he strangled and killed her.

His wife was beautiful, with dark hair that she wore pulled back in a bun and a dress that looked like it was from the pioneer days. She certainly had a haunting beauty. She conveyed to me how sad she had been that he had not believed her when, in fact, she had been telling the truth. She had loved him very much, but he would not believe her no matter how hard she tried to convince him. She was devastated in life and in death with how things had turned out. She was miserable and hopeless because nothing she said or did to reassure her husband seemed to matter. The energy I felt from her was despair.

After the murder, he carried her body and threw her into what looked like a cellar of some kind. He left the body there for a couple of days before killing himself by shooting himself in the head with a pistol. They had remained in spirit form on the earthly plane for several decades in misery and anger. They were from the area, but not necessarily from the home that they were haunting. It may surprise some people to know that ghost move around and will often follow those who are psychic. They get lonely, just like live people do and if you have any awareness of them, you are much more likely to attract them then the average person.

Once I communicated with them and learned what had happened, I explained why it would be beneficial for them to cross over. They were both afraid and I had to reassure them that they would not be punished for their actions. Many ghosts do not cross into the light because of this fear. When we commit crimes against each other, we often incarnate in another life to better understand the effects of these actions. For example, if you have killed someone, you might decide to incarnate and be killed by someone else (potentially even the one you killed previously) to get an understanding of what killing really does. To learn more about similar situations, you can read the books *Bringing Your Soul to Light* and *Your Soul's Plan*: *Discovering the Real Meaning Behind the Life You Planned Before You Were Born* by Robert Schwartz.

I also told them they could only completely heal themselves if they crossed over. They were hesitant but once I opened the light, they did cross over and it was beautiful to watch. All of their sadness, anger, and pain melted away as they walked into the light. It was so beautiful to watch them lose their pain and walk into a feeling of peace and ease as they crossed.

You Can't Take it With You

It was so beautiful for a few minutes but then the energy of the space started to feel terrible! I realized after I tuned in that all the pain and sadness that they had been holding onto had been released into the bedroom where the clearing took place. They couldn't take all that negative energy with them because you can't have that kind of energy in heaven but it had to be released somewhere, so there it was right in the room we were standing in. I promptly asked for the angels to take away that negative energy and the room immediately started to feel lighter. Imagine that all the negativity and pain they had felt after their experiences was psychic debris or energy junk and it had all just been deposited in that bedroom we were standing in! No wonder it suddenly felt terrible!

After that experience, I always start by asking the angels to protect me from any energy released by the spirits as they cross into the light. I also ask the angels to clear the energy that is released and take it away so that it doesn't remain in the space and negatively impact those who are living there. If this kinds of negative energy (or any kind of negative energy for that matter) is in someone's living space, it can literally make people sick and lead to a low functioning immune system, disease, or even death in extreme cases.

Burning sage is a great way to help remove unwanted energy though this is not always enough. I also recommend concurrently asking Archangels Michael, Raphael, Chamuel, and Jophiel to help remove any negative energy and fill it with beautiful, positive energy. Try this yourself and if you still feel negative energy, call on an expert to help bless and clear your home. Do use your intuition to determine who to hire for this type of work, or anything for that matter!

SEVEN
The Fire-starter

While most ghosts are not harmful, there are some that are. Remember, ghosts are just people without bodies, some are nice and others are not! I ran into a very unfriendly ghost while house sitting for a friend. Another friend of mine was meeting me at the house to pick me up so we could go to dinner together. He rang the doorbell and I answered and invited him in for a few minutes while I grabbed my handbag from the kitchen. Shortly after we walked into the kitchen, I heard a click and turned around and noticed the toaster oven light was on. I had not used it and had been there for several hours by myself so I was puzzled by this. I turned and walked across the kitchen to the toaster oven and when I put my hand on it, it was burning hot to the touch. I gasped and pulled my hand away in surprise and then unplugged the toaster for safety.

After that happened, I tuned in and saw that there was a male ghost who had apparently come with my friend. For those who are surprised that I didn't see him right away, it sometimes takes a certain amount of focus and effort to see ghosts. Other times, a ghost I have only felt psychically will appear very visually to me in the physical realm. I am not quite sure why that is, but I have noted it is variable. Once I focused on this ghost, it was clear that he was very unhappy. He looked like a prospector and was rough in appearance. He was very angry and threatening to me. He seemed to be afraid that I was going to try to force him to cross. Again, somehow they can tell that I have the ability to do this – I am not sure how, but it seems to be clear to spirits when they see me.

I asked him what he wanted and he basically stated that I couldn't force him to do anything and that he was very angry and threatened by me. Let me be clear that I do not usually go out of my way to get spirits to cross unless I have been hired to do so, they ask me to help them cross, or if we are living in the same space which doesn't usually work for me. Since none of these situations applied, I was a bit puzzled. He seemed determined to let me know, by preemptively attacking me, that I wasn't going to get him to do anything he didn't want to do.

Something like this had never happened before. Though I tried to reassure him that I didn't want to do anything to him that he didn't want me to do, he was very persistent and threatening towards me. I asked the angels for guidance and got that I should ask for protection for myself, for my friend, and for my belongings and the home. I did this immediately and wanted to get this spirit out of the home since he was so threatening. We left quickly and the prospector ghost came with, sitting in the back seat and threatening to burn down the house the entire time! Not only was he threatening to do this, but he kept showing me images of the house burning down to make me even more scared. I kept reassuring him I wasn't going to do anything to him that he didn't want me to do and reiterating my request to the angels for protection. He eventually left me, my belongings and my friend's home alone, but it certainly shook me up!

I do want everyone to know that if you come across a ghost that is threatening like this, you can ask for help and protection from the angels. The angels do need our permission to intervene on our behalf so be sure to ask the angels or they will just watch as things unfold. As soon as we ask (with our thoughts, in words, or in writing) this opens the door for the angels, allowing them in and giving them permission to assist. The angels can never assume what we want because we have free will, so asking is imperative. It is also important to note that by being afraid, we can create the very outcome we are afraid of! Most of our thoughts can be like unintended prayers. If we think about what we don't want, it starts to give that potential outcome energy. The angels do have the power to shift this unintentional manifestation if we ask them, so asking the angels for help repeatedly is extremely important to create big, positive shifts in our lives. The book *The Secret* helped to make this concept mainstream. You can also read more about this process and learn how to create the life of your dreams through my upcoming book *Angels & Manifesting*.

I shared this story about the ghost who threatened to start a fire because I want people to know that ghosts can cause physical harm and destruction. If I had not asked for protection for myself, my belongings, and the home in which I was staying, he very likely would have burned the house down. I am not saying this to create fear however I do want people to know this is possible. I cannot tell you how many people, when they learn what I do for a living say things like, "I don't believe in that stuff." While everyone has the right to believe what they want to, I encourage you to keep an open mind. One thing I tell those people is that just because you don't believe in *them* doesn't mean they don't believe in *you*. In other words, denying that something is there will not make it go away. However, if you recognize something is real, then you can start to learn practical tools and tips to help you when you are dealing with these types of situations. I am sure we have all done our best to simply ignore problems we've had but that can lead to the problem getting worse. It was not until I started facing my fears, ghosts, and learning about how to protect myself (and help them) that I began to feel safe. When I tried to block them out and ignore my fears, the ghosts, and other beings around me, I wound up more scared and feeling powerless.

In this field as in many others, knowledge is power. I encourage all of you to take back your feelings of power and learn about this area in a positive and empowering way. I now go into places and situations that would unnerve or even terrify most people. While I am human and I have moments of fear, I have tools to handle the situations I am placed into and am much better off than when I tried to block out my senses like the three monkeys that see no evil, hear no evil, and speak no evil. By facing what was there and learning how to handle it, I grew stronger and I am no longer ruled and controlled by the fear of the unknown like I used to be.

EIGHT
Looking for Friends

When people think of ghosts, they often think of those who have been haunting a space for a long time. They think of spirits of a different era and they might romanticize them or think of them as always being scary or sad. Sometimes they are young, they may be recent ghosts, and they can even be friendly and wanting to socialize.

I was once hired to clear a home that had several ghosts and dark entities. The family had moved there one year prior and after moving in, the family's two teenage sons' behavior had changed quite a bit. They became less motivated, their grades dropped and they had less energy. When there are entities and ghosts in a home, they can drain the occupants and distract them. When I learned about the behavioral changes, I was not terribly surprised. This all made a lot more sense once I encountered one of the ghosts in the house.

This particular spirit was spending a lot of time in the teenage boys' bedrooms. He was young, talkative, wore a sideways baseball cap and a big gold chain around his neck, and was somewhat erratic. He expressed that he'd been really happy when the family moved in because he had been looking for, in his words, "homies." He told me he was from the neighborhood, but not from that particular house. I got from the angels that he'd died in the 90's. He also told me that he'd been trying to teach both of the sons to relax and to not work so hard. He had either been a drug dealer or an addict, I was unclear which, and his death was somehow associated with drugs, though I wasn't sure why. It was no coincidence that these two young men had started having a hard time concentrating and were not motivated, because they had a male ghost in their bedrooms telling them to do just that!

You don't have to be psychic to be impacted by spirits like this. Ghosts and other energetic beings are constantly talking with us. The idea of an angel on one shoulder and a devil on the other talking to us is really not that farfetched. We often hear the words of those who are talking with us (ghosts, angels, demons, etc.) as our own thoughts. I started to have an awareness of this when I had made the decision to open up my psychic abilities and was walking down the street one day and heard in my mind, like a thought, some curse words and racial insults in reference to a person who was crossing paths with me. It sounded like my own thought, but I knew it wasn't because I do not think that way. I also felt some negative, foreign energy around me. I asked the angels to clear any beings that were not of the light and take them away from me. Do not assume that your thoughts and impulses are yours and yours alone.

In the case of this ghost and the family, they were unaware that this ghost had been talking to them, but their behavior was impacted anyway. If you have recently moved to a new home and have noticed behavioral changes in yourself or family members' behavior, it could be that a spirit, dark entity or demon is impacting you or your loved ones.

Ironically, this misguided ghost really was trying to help in his own way. He was trying to teach the young men something he knew (how to have more fun and be less serious) and he really liked them. He told me he was protective of the family and that he was really glad to have them there.

Once I'd gotten the helpful information about what this spirit had been doing there, I told him about crossing over and how that was going to be way more fun than staying there. He was unsure at first, but I kept telling him the benefits of crossing which included a lot more people to hang out with, way more fun, being able to experience just about whatever you want to over there. Since he was reluctant to leave, I explained that once he crossed, he could continue to come back any time he wanted to. I find that this helps spirits who are concerned about the process. After a little discussion, he went quickly and easily into the light.

This particular ghost stands out to me because he was friendly and trying to help, but in a way that was actually not helpful to those living there. The mother of the house in particular was quite happy to have this spirit gone and she did not find his particular brand of assistance charming or helpful.

Clearing a Space Before You Move In

The following story demonstrates the importance of clearing a space before you move in or, at the very least, before you've been there too long! It is amazing to me how we are taught to clean and clear ourselves and our spaces physically but not psychically. For example, most people wouldn't move into a home if it had trash and had not been cleaned after the previous occupants left. Now imagine that this has been happening energetically for years. Psychic debris, sadness, spirits from years past, etc. are all in a space. When you move in, you are moving in not only with the ghosts and their baggage, but also all the energetic cast-offs from the physical occupants as well. This can be quite a mess. This sets me up to tell you the story about the next chapter and how the history of a place is so important when considering a move. There is some clearing that can be done for spaces but if there have been intense things that happened in a place or burial grounds that have been disturbed, this can make it a challenging place to live.

For this reason, I recommend following your intuition about whether to purchase a home or move into an area. I also recommend that you ask the angels to clear any energy or energy beings that are not beneficial and hire an expert to help for more challenging situations.

NINE
The Gentlemanly Ghost

I occasionally work with Altitude Paranormal Group, a Denver based paranormal group. I have done home investigations and investigated many very haunted and fascinating sites, but one of my favorite locations was the Old Louisiana State Capitol Building in Louisiana. Many people do not realize that though New Orleans was the capital of the Orleans territory, the seat of government was moved to Baton Rouge in 1849 and it has remained there since then. The current state capitol building was built in 1931 and opened in 1932. The original capitol opened in 1849. Both buildings have dramatic histories however I've only had the pleasure of experiencing the intrigue and drama of the original capitol building.

It had over a decade of use before the civil war broke out, and was an active location during the war itself. It was used as a prison for the union army. Then in 1862 it caught fire and went into disrepair and was even used as a mechanics institute. It was later reconstructed in 1882 and the current beautiful spiral staircase and stained glass windows were added. It once again became the seat of government.

Note: Photos in print are black and white and may not be as clear as in electronic form. Electronic photos can be seen clearly in the kindle version, which can be purchased economically through the Amazon Matchstick Program.

Old Louisiana State Capitol Building Exterior
Photo by Laura Powers

Interior of the Old Louisiana State Capitol Building
Photo by Laura Powers

I was there with Marisa and Grayson from the Altitude Paranormal Group. Because we need privacy in order to know that any evidence we receive is not created by live people, we got there very early in the morning before 6 a.m. The building currently operates as a museum so we had to be done with our investigation before it was open to the public at 8:30 or 9 a.m. We knew from talking with our contact at the museum that there was definite spirit activity there. The only others besides ourselves were the security crew who showed up part way through the investigation in the basement and our contact who had a separate office in the basement. We had the place to ourselves for a good couple of hours before the museum staff and attendees arrived.

I was there with Marisa, a petite and sweet young woman with a good nature and naturally good looks. Grayson, originally a Louisiana native, started and runs Altitude Paranormal Group from Denver, Colorado. Being a smart man, Grayson has noticed that oftentimes ghosts, particularly male ghosts, are more likely to interact with women than men. This is something I think producers of paranormal shows might pay attention to since most of the paranormal shows out there feature mostly men. After all, male ghosts are still men and they do, generally speaking, like women. Given this predilection, Grayson asked Marisa and me to work together and he worked alone.

She and I went into one of the rooms that was currently an exhibit room but had previously been offices when the seat of government had been there. As soon as we walked into the room I could sense a presence. Before we had even set up our equipment, which in this case was a video recorder, an audio recorder, a flashlight, and a small plastic ball, I saw the ghost of a man. He was quite friendly and talkative, in fact he had an ambassador-like energy. He seemed happy to see us and wanted to tell us all about the building. He immediately wanted to take us to the basement. I expressed to him that we weren't ready to go down there yet because we had planned to stay in that room for 30 minutes, and if we moved too soon and made noise, Grayson might mistake any noises we made as coming from paranormal activity.

He was disappointed as he clearly wanted to go down there right then. He even started to walk down there himself but once he saw that we weren't following him, he returned and stayed with us. He talked a lot and while I am somewhat clairaudient (hearing psychically); my strongest senses are clairvoyance (visual) and clairsentience (feeling). I can see spiritual beings, receive their intention, and see what they are trying to show me. He showed me how he used to work there and it was clear that he knew he was a spirit. He liked hanging out there and had no desire to cross into the light. He was just excited we were there and was going to take the opportunity to share with us what he had experienced. I could see him very clearly down to the details and based on the style of his dress, he had clearly been a ghost for a very long time. He was most definitely a gentleman and wore a type of suit that was similar to ones Mark Twain was known to wear. Interestingly, I learned later that Mark Twain had been a steamboat pilot on the Mississippi river and once said of the Old Louisiana State Capitol Building, "It is pathetic....that whitewashed castle, with turrets and things.....should never have been built in this otherwise honorable place."

One of the things that I found interesting is that not only did he know he was a ghost, but he also was quite clear on why we were there. Since he had been a ghost for quite some time, he could manipulate matter and energy quite well.

For those who don't know much about paranormal investigation, there are many tools that are used to document and communicate with paranormal beings. Below is a list of basic paranormal investigation tools and how they are used.

Paranormal Investigation Toolkit

- Audio recorder

- Manually adjustable twist flashlight
- Lightweight plastic ball
- Camera
- Video camera
- EMF (Electro Magnetic Frequency) reader
- Motion sensors
- Infrared sensing equipment (heat sensitive)
- Ghost Box or Spirit Box (scans radio frequencies)

Audio recorders are used to record the session and capture EVPs (Electronic Voice Phenomenon). If you'd like to learn more about electronic voice phenomenon in general, you can look up the American Association of Electronic Phenomenon, a non-profit whose sole focus is EVPs. It is important, when listening to any recordings, not to disregard the recording right away even if you don't hear anything with your naked ear. Oftentimes, the volume of the sound must be bumped up quite a bit in order to hear spirit communication. One mistake that novice investigators often make is to talk too much and not give the spirit time to respond. Remember if you are trying to have a communication and it's a two way street. If you talk the whole time, then they will likely not be heard. The best recordings I have listened to were given to an expert audio engineer who removed background noises and static and then increased the volume and clarity of any paranormal voices or noises captured. I have heard some incredible EVPs captured with simple audio recorders that you can buy for $50.

A flashlight may seem like a silly and low tech tool to use for paranormal investigation, but in fact, it can be quite helpful as a communication tool. I am talking about the small flashlights that twist on and twist off. This allows the spirits to use their energy to manipulate the flashlight and turn it on and off. Paranormal investigators often use these to communicate with ghosts and ask questions that the ghosts can answer by turning the flashlight on and off.

Lightweight plastic balls are used because it is possible for spirits to manipulate physical matter. These kinds of balls can be moved by spirits. Not surprisingly, child spirits, are more likely to want to interact in this way.

A camera can be used to take photos of spirits. In very rare cases, a full apparition will appear in a photo. More commonly, orbs will appear. Orbs that are solid, are colored, or have clear movement are harder to dismiss as dust particles. Another fascinating thing I have learned about orbs that appear in photos, is that they can appear long after the photo was taken. I have looked at a photo just after it was taken, and no orbs appeared, yet later orbs were in the picture. I have included a few examples of photos I have taken that included orbs or spirit phenomenon. The photos at the Salem Cemetery are notable because there are several orbs, one of which is opaque and bright. The photos taken at the Historic Plains Hotel were only a small selection from several that I took. The one with a railing has several bright orbs and what appears to be an apparition in front of the elevator door with an orb right in its center. The one of the corner shows a streaking orb. The Glenwood Springs Fairy Cave photo shows several orbs, one of which has a bright green color. As a psychic medium, I used my gifts to decide when to take a photo so I often get orbs in my photos when others don't. I also get many photos with orbs in them since there is always a lot of spirit activity around me. I've included a photo of me on a motorcycle with a bright orb near my head as an example.

Orbs at the Salem Cemetery in Walker, Louisiana
Photo by Laura Powers

Orbs and an apparition (a woman in a dress on the elevator door) at the Historic Plains Hotel in Cheyenne, Wyoming
Photo by Laura Powers

Moving, opaque white orb at the Historic Plains Hotel in Cheyenne, Wyoming
Photo by Laura Powers

Orbs at the Fairy Caves in Glenwood Springs, Colorado
Photo by Laura Powers

Orb photo with Laura Powers outside of the Milk Nightclub in Denver, Colorado
Photo courtesy Laura Powers

Video cameras can document movement, voices, and unusual spirit activity. Be warned that oftentimes spirits like to mess with equipment in unexpected ways. Sometimes they may delete footage or drain batteries. I was at an investigation with Altitude Paranormal at a residential home in Centennial, Colorado where there was significant spirit activity and both my regular camera and another investigator's video camera were drained from full battery to shutting off in about two minutes. I know that this was very purposeful. These spirits did not want us there and they were making it as difficult as possible for us, and trying to get us to leave.

An EMF (Electro Magnetic Frequency) reader or meter detects changes in energy fields. When there is a spike in an energy field it can be from a spirit though Wi-Fi signals and other frequencies can also interfere with a reading. When an EMF reader suddenly spikes from a low reading to a high reading when the meter has not moved locations, it's often a sign of paranormal activity.

Motion sensors can be set up and are often triggered by spirits. Video cameras can be set to document that there is nothing physical triggering the sensor. I have seen this happen several times.

Infrared cameras, or similar equipment, identify heat markers. Areas of coolness for example are usually indicative of ghosts. In my experience angels bring in a lot of heat, especially Archangel Michael. When he comes in, it can feel like someone turned the heat on!

Ghost or spirit boxes are devices that scan radio frequencies to pick up signals. Spirits will use these frequencies to communicate. Only in very rare cases is there DVP (Direct-Voice Phenomena) which is when a spirit communicates directly through voice without the use of technology or a psychic medium.

Now that you understand the tools we had at our disposal, you can understand how incredible what happened next was. We were communicating with this gentleman spirit through the use of a flashlight and asking him questions. Usually yes/no questions work best with these kinds of flashlights. We said out loud, "Did you work here in the building, if yes please turn on the flashlight." The flashlight flickered on and then dimmed indicating a yes response. We asked him many other questions as well as asking that he speak to us through the recorder.

The entire time we were doing this he expressed impatience and wanted to go downstairs. I would later learn why. As we were nearing the end of our timed 30 minutes, Marisa asked him if he died in the building. Just after that, all the lights in the room were turned on at once and the flashlight remained dim. I believe that was the spirit answering us in a more dramatic fashion than the flashlight allowed. We learned later that the lights in the building were on a timer and they had come on only in that room several minutes earlier than the timer programming. Also we were the only people present in that room.

Throughout the entire session, we heard doors slamming open and closed in the remainder of the building. We assumed that employees must have been doing it as the sound was so incredibly loud. We felt we could identify that the sound was coming from the doors that were on the floors above the winding central staircase. The doors were about 8 feet tall, metal, and very heavy. After we finished our investigation, we were told by our contact that he had been monitoring the cameras throughout the building and he confirmed that no one had been on those floors. No living person could have slammed the doors. The evidence in that particular case was astounding.

After checking some other spaces that proved less exciting, we went to the basement. Our gentleman spirit friend followed us part way down and then stated he didn't want to go any farther. He indicated to me that he didn't like the security guards who were there; by this time the museum was close to opening and they were on duty. Now I knew why he had wanted us to go down earlier. He wanted to show us the basement, but he had wanted to do it before the security guards arrived.

We learned that there had been a lot of activity recently in the basement. This was not surprising since that was where the prison and makeshift hospital were during the civil war. Wherever there are people dying, imprisoned or in pain, spirit activity often increases and the energy of these moments and experiences can also leave a sort of energy imprint on the space. Interestingly, we did have some activity on the EMF readers and we sensed some pockets of cold activity, but mostly it felt quiet while we were there. That doesn't mean that there wasn't activity, the spirits either may not have been there at that exact moment, or they may have chosen not to interact with us. Remember that they can move around, just as we can.

After we had completed our investigation, we were told the story of State Senator Pierre Couvillon who died in 1851 while in a heated debate, presumably of a heart attack, on the Senate floor. When I saw the sketch of him and description, I immediately believed that the gentlemanly ghost we had spoken to was Pierre Couvillon. I do love it when I get an image of a spirit or ghost and then find historical evidence that matches what I have seen psychically - and this was definitely one of those cases. I enjoyed our conversation very much and would very much like to chat with him again and perhaps go to the basement with him to see what it was that he wanted so badly to show me.

Pierre Couvillon Sketch at the Old Louisiana State Capitol Building
Photo by Laura Powers

As we were leaving the site, we took a photo of the team outside of the capitol building and the photo displays an unusual phenomenon that could be an apparition. While I am not a photography expert, I have shown the photo to professional photographers and have been told the photo is not lens flare, dust, etc. Given the lighting and environment, what is captured in the photo is not likely to be caused by anything easily explained. I've included the photo below so you can judge for yourself. You can also read an article about the difference between lens flare and apparitions here: http://www.ishootshows.com/2011/07/13/understanding-lens-flare-ghosting/.

Marisa, Grayson and Laura from Altitude Paranormal Group
Outside the Old Louisiana State Capitol Building
Photo courtesy Laura Powers

TEN
Lions and Tigers and Bears

I am not going to actually talk about lions and tigers and bears, but I do want to share a few personal stories I have had with my work relating to animal ghosts. While humans have spirits, or more accurately, while spirits incarnate as humans, they often do as animals too! For the most part, there are spirits that tend to incarnate as humans and those that tend to incarnate as animals, with some crossover. It is entirely possible for one who was incarnated as an animal to later incarnate as a human and vice versa. I realize that some people may find this troubling, given how we treat animals in our society today. If you'd like to learn more about this topic, you can read Rob Schwartz's book *Your Soul's Plan: Discovering the Real Meaning of the Life You Planned Before You Were Born* which has some information on the topic.

Even though I know that there are animal ghosts, they still sometimes surprise me! I'll share a few stories of my interactions with animal spirits. Animal ghosts tend to be less aggressive with humans than human ghosts; there are some that can be actually quite sweet!

The Mounted Elk

I have never liked mounted animal heads very much, unless they are carved out of wood or otherwise fake and now I know why. When doing clearing work at a ranch, I walked into their den to see the ghost of an elk standing there. He was sad and forlorn. Obviously he felt out of place. I focused and began telepathic communication with him. He showed me how he had been standing out in a field and the next moment he was looking at his body as it was being dressed after the hunt. He had died but it happened so quickly and without warning, that he didn't understand what had happened. When I spoke with the family about this, they explained that he had been shot from far away. Animals that are killed with long range shot guns like this can experience confusion because they don't have any conscious explanation for what has happened. If they are chased in the wild by a predator, they will have their fear response triggered. They will understand on a deep level that they were in danger. When they are shot from a great distance, this doesn't happen. If they are killed quickly, it can lead to great confusion as to what has happened.

Not knowing what else to do, this poor elk stayed with what was left of him after the slaughter, his mounted head. I am sure it felt very unnatural for him to hang out in this family's den, but he didn't know what else to do. I felt for the poor elk, hanging out there with humans totally lost outside of his natural environment. I opened up the light for him to cross and he too was greeted by family members who were waiting to escort him into the light. I felt his relief and happiness when he was greeted by his loved ones. After he crossed, the den felt much lighter and brighter without the spirit of the lost and sad elk standing there. If you do not like being around preserved animals or you feel sad around them, there is the possibility that there is still the spirit of the animal nearby.

Ghost Cats

In my experience, kitties tend to make more ghosts than dogs do. Perhaps cats have a harder time letting go? I am not really sure, but I can tell you that I have had the spirits of several kitties visit and even live with me as ghosts. Usually ghost kitties are not sad, angry or frustrated like their human counterparts. Based on my experience, these spirit kitties simply like to stay where they are and visit the places and people they knew when they were alive. I've had several encounters with ghost kitties and they were very sweet, often jumping on my bed, purring and "kneading biscuits" with their paws in a sign of contentment.

Whenever I sense one of them there, I always open up the light to give them the opportunity to cross if they are ready. The energy coming from ghost kitties is resoundingly more positive than the energy coming from most human ghosts, which I think says a lot about the human perspective. Most humans are more sad and unhappy than their animal counterparts. The upside of our large, analytical brains is the ability to analyze and think in objective terms but that is also our challenge. Most animals are less likely to get wrapped up in day-to-day concerns and are content to be in the moment. When I come across a ghost cat, I do help them cross but there is not usually the same sense of sadness and desperation with them. Ghost cats also usually do not feed on a person's energy the way that human ones do, so this means not only is the ghost in a better space but the people living around the ghost are not as negatively affected. Because of this there is, in my opinion, less urgency to help them cross since they are not detrimental to others.

The Coyote Pelt

Just as a spirit can be attached to a mounted head, a spirit can also remain attached to another part of its body including its pelt. When a client handed me a coyote pelt, I knew immediately that the coyote spirit was still there and was not at peace. The family that had the pelt had received it from the man who had hunted it. I put the pelt in my lap and the feeling was as if I was holding a sad, sick, and frightened dog. I held the pelt there, and stroked it and opened up the light, asking the coyote's angels and spirit guides to assist. Who came through surprised me. Given my human form and that my clients are human, most of the spirits I've helped cross are human, so I don't have nearly as much experience helping animal spirits cross. Also, there seem to be fewer animal ghosts than human ghosts in my experience. I was therefore surprised when one of the coyote's spirit guides stepped forward. He was a Native American man and he was there comforting and assisting the coyote into the light. The spirit of the coyote crossed into the light and I could feel his joy as he was released. I can only imagine what that must have felt like for him to be trapped here.

He had shown me how he used to howl at the moon and run and had felt so alive! Then he'd been shot and had not understood what had happened. Like the elk, he stayed with his body (or what was left of it) since he didn't know what else to do. The family who received the pelt was storing it in a trunk and it felt suffocating for him. They actually told me they felt the pelt was sad. How right they were! To be a coyote who was accustomed to running and playing in the wild and then to be attached to a pelt being stored in a piece of furniture was no way to exist. If you have negative feelings about a fur, bones, or any other item that used to be a part of an animal, it is possible that the spirit of the animal may be attached and therefore not at peace. Another possibility is that the object could have absorbed negative energy associated with the trauma of the animal or previous owners or environments. Ask the angels to clear any residual energy and help the spirit cross into the light if there is a spirit attached.

Helping the coyote was a learning experience for me and helped me understand how connected we all are. Just as humans can have animal spirit guides, so too can animals have human spirit guides. We truly are in this together to help each other out. After the spirit of the animal had crossed into the light, the angels instructed me to have the family bury the pelt out of honor and respect, which they did. Finally this coyote was at peace.

Animal Communication

I am not an animal communicator but there are times when live animals communicate with me. When they do the communication can be quite striking! Once after doing some clearing work at the Sand Creek Massacre Site (more on that later) an animal reached out to me in a surprising way. I was driving back with my team on a rural highway. It was nearing nightfall; it was winter and very, very cold. We were travelling at about 75 miles an hour when we passed a cattle field. There were several cows standing by the road but one in particular reached out telepathically to communicate with me. Just like ghosts, animals can sometimes tell who has psychic gifts.

Her consciousness connected with mine and she expressed sadness and concern that they were disregarded by humans. She essentially told me, "Hey, we get cold. We have feelings!" This cow was practically yelling at me, psychically speaking. The fact that she was expressing this to me means that she recognized that most humans don't get this. We think that some animals are unfeeling and almost unconscious which is simply not true.

I communicated back to her that I was sorry and I would let people know. I believe it is easier for people to disregard animals as unfeeling because we know that we don't treat them well. It is easier to deal with the guilt we have as a society by pretending that the animals we are subjecting to terrible conditions don't feel. I hope that those reading this will recognize that animals are conscious and have souls as well. We tend to think that way for our pets, but not always for farm animals. I ask the angels regularly to help with the treatment of all animals on this planet and recommend you do too! Animals deserve to be treated with dignity and respect, just like their human counterparts.

ELEVEN
The Most Haunted Park in Denver

There is a park in my home state that is famous for how haunted it is. When you learn the history of the place, you can understand why! Cheesman Park is located in Denver which is considered a Wild West town. Colorado (then a territory) was fairly sparsely populated until the gold rush. It was the silver rush that got lots of people moving out west. The infamous Molly Brown, dubbed the "Unsinkable Molly Brown" from having escaped the sinking Titanic, made her fortune from the silver mining rush. Denver and the surrounding areas developed very quickly and as a result, crime was rampant and there were a lot of rough characters around. Life was hard, there was disease, living conditions were challenging, and men often found comfort in the arms of prostitutes and gambled their fortunes away in gambling halls.

But western miners weren't the first people to live there. There were several Native American tribes that had settled in what is now Denver and the surrounding areas, long before white people came there. Most people know that when the white settlers came, they often displaced those that were already there and it was often bloody. When this displacement happened, not only were the living moved, but sometimes the dead were too. Native American burial grounds and sacred sites were often taken over in very disrespectful ways. This type of thing can really rile up ghosts whose bodies were in those burial grounds.

Let me first say that most cemeteries are in fact pretty peaceful, but there are some cemeteries that are quite active. Places that formerly were cemeteries and have been turned into something else will often have a lot of unhappy, displaced spirits in them. The whole Front Range in Colorado as well as many places in Mexico and Wyoming are filled with these kinds of places. Most people do not even think about the spiritual and energetic ramifications of living in a place that has this kind of history, particularly if the changes made to the land happened decades or centuries ago. Time does not pass for ghosts in the same way and they may haunt for decades or centuries with passion. If the spirits were displaced, they are likely to be very unhappy about this and if you buy a home in a former burial ground, you may have some very unhappy spirits on your hands!

I've had several interactions with this park myself. I've spent time there for Pride Festival parade line-up, been hired by a client to clear a home, done some pro-bono clearing work in the park, and tuned into the park with a class doing remote viewing (looking at a place psychically from a remote location), and each time there was a lot of activity.

The Never Ending Battle

The remote viewing exercise was fascinating. As a class, we tuned into the park and I was amazed at what I saw. The ghosts of Native Americans and pioneers were fighting in seemingly endless battle for territory in the park. After all, when a battle does not end because you can't die, what do you do? These spirits were so locked into confrontation that they were literally never going to have any peace if left to their own devices. When I get hired to clear a space, it often means that I am spending lots of one-on-one time with each spirit. In cases like this, that would take an enormous amount of time! Ghosts also have to make the decision to want to shift. So instead, we as a class, opened up the light as a vehicle for those who were ready to transition into the after-life. I am sure some did but many of them were too caught up in their struggles and fighting to let go and cross. When you do this work it is easy to feel overwhelmed with the amount of work that needs to be done so it is important to choose your battles, so to speak.

Peeping Tom

I had been hired by a client who lived near the park to clear her home of activity. There were several dark entities we cleared there. One was an oozy entity that dripped energetic goo and gave her bad dreams. The room in particular had stagnant energy and the breeze rarely moved through. The being that stands out the most from that particular clearing job, though, was a male ghost who has been there since the pioneer days. He was definitely a womanizer, and one of the things he really enjoyed doing that he hadn't been able to do while alive without beings seen or caught was spying on women. I was shown that he regularly spied on the female client when she was in the shower. She told me she had felt watched. If you are feeling watched and there is no one physically there, it is very likely that a spirit is watching you.

As it turned out, though this spirit liked to spy on his live house-mate, he really was a romantic at heart and one of the reasons he hadn't crossed was he was looking for his love. Given that he had been a ghost for over a century and his love wasn't with him, I was fairly sure his love was in the after-life. I told him that and he listened fairly easily. I told him what I often tell spirits who are unsure, which is that if they go to the after-life and they don't find who or what they are looking for, they can always come back (they almost never do). He agreed. He crossed fairly quickly but not without cheekily looking back at myself and the client and giving us a wolfish grin before he crossed into the light.

Wild Weather

After the house clearing in the area, I decided to go and do some pro-bono clearing work in the park. I could feel the activity so I thought I might as well go see what I could do. It was in August and it was a warm summer day with a mellow breeze. I went with my friend, Jan. She and I left my client and drove a few blocks to the Cheesman Park and parked the car. We walked around and felt the energy of the area. I actually only directly interacted with one spirit, a woman who was wearing a beautiful dress and a bustle. She was friendly and felt relatively happy enjoying the park. Even though she's the only spirit I interacted with, I could feel that the park was filled with activity.

Since I didn't have hours and hours to spend connecting with and crossing the spirits individually, I decided to take a different approach. When I open up the light for one spirit to cross, I normally open a fairly small pillar of light; say big enough for a few people to walk through. Cheesman Park is a large park, approximately 81 acres according to Google. In order to allow as many earth bound spirits to cross at a time, I focused and opened the light around the entire circumference of the park. This is the largest circle of light to date I have ever opened. As soon as I did this a huge gust of wind swept up and whirled around me. I could feel a huge and sudden energy shift.

I walked around briefly and then felt that it was time to go. Jan and I walked to the car and headed home. I was living in Lafayette, Colorado at the time, which is about 33 miles from Denver and the park. We noticed some clouds gathering in the sky. As we drove, they started to look more and more ominous. Since we had quite a drive, we watched the clouds build and the sky darken. By the time we made it to Lafayette, the wind was whipping the tree branches and we could tell that a downpour was imminent. I said goodbye to Jan hastily and I ran from the car to my house right before the sky seemed to open up and the rain started to pour down in huge droplets that made loud thudding sounds as they hit the pavement. Even though I had only a short distance to go, I was nearly soaked through by the time I got to my front door.

I went inside and toweled off, and got into some comfy clothes. I was starving and warmed up some food to eat. Often times after doing this kind of work, I am ravenous and will not get my energy back until I've eaten. I was also exhausted. Even though it was only late afternoon, I was suddenly so tired I could barely keep my eyes open. I crawled into bed and fell into a deep and heavy sleep. I woke up about three hours later, ate some more and went to sleep. I woke up 12 hours later. Even though physically, I'd hardly done anything that day, I had done a ton energetically so it was not surprising that I needed so much rest. It was kind of like moving a mountain; essentially I'd moved a mountain of energy that afternoon. I do charge quite a bit for this work but that is largely because it is not just about the time and energy that I spend physically on the activity. It is not uncommon to be totally wiped out energetically after doing a clearing. Like many things, I have gotten stronger at this work with practice. Our psychic abilities strengthen just like our physical ones do, so I am much stronger and have more stamina now after doing this work for several years. Even after lots of practice, I can get wiped out if what I am dealing with is particularly intense.

Later the following day, I heard about all of the crazy weather that had occurred the previous afternoon. There had been crazy and unseasonal hail and torrential rain in Denver. Intense winds had even destroyed a velodrome (a wooden bicycle track). You can read more about this on the 303 cycling website: http://303cycling.com/erie-velodrome-takes-on-damage-after-storm. I have always felt the strong connection between the energy and the weather but this was one of the most extreme examples. I've noticed many times that storm clouds roll in after I've done my clearing work.

I was rather puzzled by this phenomenon until I read the book *Weather Shamanism: Harmonizing our Connection with the Elements* by Nan Moss and David Corbin. It is a book that deals with many different aspects of the energy and consciousness of weather. In the book, one of the theories mentioned is that weather was like the immune system for the planet. Suddenly this made sense to me! I had directly experienced the negative energy that could be released when earth bound spirits crossed into the light. Now I understood that when the negative energy is released, especially en masse, the earth needs to clear it. One way to do that was weather. Wind and water literally blew and cleared these negative energy accumulations away. It was brilliant really! Since the clearing I did in Cheesman Park was so large, I just wasn't prepared for the sheer amount of energy that was released. I was also equally unprepared for the reaction from Mother Nature to clear the energy themselves. In retrospect it all makes sense and I am a bit more cautious with doing clearings this large now. If I do, then I will at least be prepared for the resulting reaction!

I do also recommend asking the angels to help clear the energy that is released as well but if there is a large influx like this; Mother Nature may kick in before the angels get the energy cleared out. Kind of like if you ingested something toxic, the body might immediately expel it by vomiting. This planet is most definitely alive and she takes care of herself in ways that we do not always understand.

Needless to say I have never looked at weather the same way again after that experience. I am sure there are those who would say that these are unrelated incidents, but I know psychically that they were connected. Since then I have experienced other times when the weather was affected by crossing spirits into the light but I will never forget how dramatic that afternoon in August was.

TWELVE
Movie Time

Did you know that many ghosts enjoy the same things that we do? This can include even some unlikely pastimes! I learned this one night when I was out with a friend of mine for a late movie. He and I often went to movies later in the evening and this night was no exception. We had chosen the movie *Insidious: Chapter 2* for that particular evening. For those who don't know, *Insidious: Chapter 2* is the sequel to the original movie *Insidious* which tells the tale of a boy who struggles with his body being used as a vessel for spirits. I was actually surprised when I was guided to see this movie and another movie *The Conjuring* because they are so dark, but sometimes the angels will send me to a movie for research.

Insidious: Chapter 2 has a portrayal of a psychic medium; it is always interesting for me to see how Hollywood depicts people who do what I do. It is a pretty intense movie that features ghosts, dark entities and possession. It is definitely not for the faint of heart! Note if you do go to a movie that is scary or has intense themes, I highly recommend calling Archangel Michael and the angels to protect you energetically and physically as there are dark entities and demons that feed on fear and anxiety which these types of movies tend to produce! They can even cause physical damage if you are unprotected.

My friend and I went to the movie at a Cherry Creek movie theater at 11 pm. Since it was a late show, the audience consisted only of my friend, one other couple, and me. The other couple was towards the front of the theater and my friend and I were sitting in the very back row. We had a clear view of the entire theater from there. The movie is an edge-of-your seat kind of movie, so I wasn't really looking around at the theater much once the film started. About half-way through the movie, my friend got up to get a refill on his drink. This broke me out of my focus, and when I glanced over to watch him exit our row. I was shocked to see the ghost of a man sitting just two seats away from my friend. He was Caucasian, middle aged, and he continued to watch the movie even as I observed him. I was surprised for many reasons. I had never seen a ghost at a movie before. Usually ghosts express some active interest in me and he did not. I thought his choice of movie was highly ironic given that it was about ghosts interacting with live people. Since he didn't seem to be causing any problems, I let him continue watching the movie and I did the same.

A short time later, my friend returned to his seat with his freshly refilled drink. My friend was also very psychic, so when he sat down, I asked if he had felt anything unusual when he went to get his drink. He said he had felt some coolness when he walked away and again when he came back. I told him he had walked right through the energy field of a ghost a couple of seats over. Thankfully, since he had some paranormal experience, he wasn't scared the way many people might have been!

We watched the rest of the movie in peace and when my friend and I left after the credits, the ghost was still sitting there. I still get a laugh at that situation and wondered what brought him to that particular movie!

THIRTEEN
The Sand Creek Massacre

Occasionally a spirit will come to me and ask for help assisting other spirits. This happened to me in late November of 2012 when a Native American spirit came to me to help earth bound spirits that had become trapped and were in continual terror at the site of the Sand Creek Massacre in Colorado on November 29, 1864. The spirit asked me to help these poor souls who were in such a desperate place after dying in such a traumatic way. Though I'd heard of the Sand Creek Massacre, I didn't know much about it, so I did some research to help me understand what happened before I went there.

The massacre occurred during the Civil War during a critical time in Native American and American government relations. Members of the Cheyenne and Arapaho tribes were camped on land in the Colorado territory (it would become a state in 1876) in an area near the present-day city of Eads. Those at the encampment had been promised safety if they kept the peace, and flew the US flag. One of the leaders was

Black Kettle, a Cheyenne chief. I believe it was Chief Black Kettle who came to me in spirit form to ask for help. He was not a ghost but a spirit in the light who wanted to help his people.

Chief Black Kettle
Source: Wikipedia

He was an advocate of peace and was known for working to come to agreements with white settlers rather than fighting. He travelled all the way from their territory (present day Kansas and Colorado) to see President Lincoln to express his intentions to be at peace. Lincoln was receptive and gave him a US flag. Despite his best efforts, brutal military action is what came instead of the peace he desired. Black Kettle had also met with the Governor of the Colorado territory, John Evans as well as with Colonel Chivington who was in charge of the military forces in Colorado.

John Evans made a public proclamation that set the ball rolling and led to the Sand Creek Massacre. According to Wikipedia, John Evans made the following statement: *authorizing "all citizens of Colorado . . . to go in pursuit of all hostile Indians [and] kill and destroy all enemies of the country." Evans ordered that so-called "friendly" "Indians" should present themselves to various forts for their "safety and protection," and those who did not were "hostile" and should be "pursued and destroyed."*

Later that year, Colonel Chivington mobilized approximately 700 cavalry with the specific intent to decimate the settlement. They marched nearly 200 miles from Denver to the settlement on horseback simply for this purpose. The night of the attack, they drank and celebrated their victory in advance. After the march the soldiers arrived at the settlement while most of the Native American men were out hunting. This meant that when the troops arrived, there was no one to protect the women, children and elders. It really and truly was a slaughter.

The troops were vicious and they scalped and brutally slayed those they came upon. Bodies were dismembered and parts of them were kept as souvenirs by some of the soldiers. It was a devastating experience for the Native Americans. Given the circumstances and the trauma surrounding their deaths, it is not surprising that many of those who were killed did not cross into the light and became earth-bound spirits or ghosts. Many of these ghosts were literally trapped in the terror of what had happened to them, reliving the nightmare over and over again. Because time does not pass in the same way for ghosts, this literally stretched on for decades. I also learned from the angels that many of the troops and especially Colonel Chivington were being strongly influenced by demons and dark entities. After those from the settlement were slaughtered, more demons and dark entities came and fed on the pain, sorrow and horror of those who had died. Since these dark beings feed on energy, it didn't matter to them that the bodies had died; they could continue to feed on the energy of these individuals in perpetuity, as long as the ghosts were trapped in the material plane.

After doing a little bit of research on the events, I planned to go to help those spirits that I could. I asked my good friend Jan, as well as my friend Alesa, to come with me to assist and help with the video. I knew this was not going to be emotionally easy so I was glad to have two close friends with me.

Alesa and I had been friends since before we were both divorced. We used to play Texas Hold 'Em on our driveways together with our husbands at the time. Even though our lives were very different, we grew to be very close after our lives shifted and we found that we were kindred spirits. Alesa is an angel and a total sweetheart with a heart of gold, and a beautiful smile. She is one of those friends who offers no judgment and has my back no matter what. When I bring people with me, I like to make sure they are energetically in a good place and are open to what I do. When people are skeptical, it can block the flow of information.

Alesa, Jan and I arranged to go as soon as our schedules allowed. As it turned out, we would be there almost exactly 148 years after the massacre took place as we went on December 1st and the massacre had happened on November 29th.

The morning of the trip arrived and we made our way towards Eads, Colorado and the Sand Creek Massacre site. It is nearly a four hour drive so we got an early start. Nearly the entire drive there, I was fielding off attacks on myself and my friends. One entity attacked Jan's hip so badly that we had to pull over. It was exhausting and we hadn't even gotten to the site yet. We stopped only to stretch our legs and to get tea and coffee at a truck stop. Several hours later we arrived.

The site truly is in a rural area so once you get away from the parking area of the memorial, it is easy to imagine it as it was so many decades ago. The landscape in this area, in December, is pretty barren. It was mostly grasses and scrub brushes and a line of trees near Sand Creek itself. You can see photos on the National Park Service Site: http://www.nps.gov/nr/travel/cultural_diversity/Sand_Creek_Massacre_National_Historic_Site.html.

The parking area was calm and quiet and we collected ourselves and our belongings and made our way and walked towards the site itself. As soon as we were in the site itself, I immediately sensed a presence. I psychically tuned in, closed my eyes and saw the spirit of Chief Black Kettle before me. He was so wise and filled me with a sense of peace. He expressed great gratitude that I had come and held his palms out to me in a welcoming gesture. In the center of his hands something glowed. The light was so bright; I couldn't see what it was emanating from. Perhaps he was showing me light itself. Whatever it was he was offering it to me. I was very honored and thanked him. He smiled at me and gestured for me to continue on my way and showed me that he would be there with me.

Feeling incredibly touched by the welcome and gratitude I had felt from Chief Black Kettle, I made my way down the path with my friends, towards the site of the attack. The site itself has a memorial building, a tipi and a marked path that goes up over the crest of a hill. On the other side of the hill is the creek and the site where the majority of the massacre happened. It was a warm and quiet day for December. It was windy but it was not snowing as it might have been. At one point, a butterfly flew in front of us, flying upwards towards the path and in the direction we were walking. It was as it if was showing us the way. I did not even think about it at the time as it felt so natural but looking back on it, I cannot remember ever seeing another butterfly in December in Colorado. It was a little miracle for us that day. When I see butterflies, they are always for me a symbol of beauty, transformation and rebirth. This was the perfect message from nature for us.

We made our way up the dusty trail and the first earth-bound spirit was that of one of the warriors. At one time, I would have referred to him as a brave but now I know that term is not appropriate for all tribes and some find it offensive. This man was young, with long hair in braids. He showed me that he had been killed early on in the massacre. He was so sad that he had not been able to protect his people. I felt overwhelmed with his grief and sadness. I also deeply felt his disappointment at not having been able to protect his loved ones. I honored what he felt and listened to him; often-times spirits that are trapped simply need someone to hear them and to honor their experience. I opened up the light to the other-side and watched as he crossed. Immediately the grief and sadness I had been feeling melted away as he crossed over. It is always such a relief and a wonderful feeling to witness those who are in pain and suffering transition to a peaceful place.

We continued up the path until I felt another spirit. This one had a completely different energy. He was off the path and farther off from the others I sensed ahead. As we got closer I realized why. This was a soldier. No wonder he didn't want to spend time with the other spirits there. As a soldier, he did not fit in, nor were the spirits of the Cheyenne and Arapaho likely to welcome him. He kept his distance. I wanted to learn his story so he showed me that he had ridden in on a horse with the rest of the troops. As he had gotten closer, he had dismounted. He communicated surprise and dismay and what he had found when he arrived. He had expected a battle, not to be killing women and children. He did not fight. He got off his horse and was confused about what to do when he was hit on the back of the head and killed. He never saw who did it; though I am sure it was someone from one of the tribes there - with good reason. Nevertheless, I felt sorry for him. He was clearly misinformed about what the plan was, when he got there, he wanted no part of it. He was immediately killed and had been lost and confused for almost 150 years since. He was not angry, simply dismayed at the circumstances he found himself in. I explained that I could help him cross over to the other side. I opened up the light and helped him cross. He crossed quickly and was quite relieved to be away from the entire situation. While I always go in open minded, I am often surprised by the circumstances the ghosts show me and he certainly was no exception.

After helping him cross, we continued to walk up the hill, hit the crest and started our descent towards the tree line and the creek itself. The energy got heavier and the air seemed to thicken. We seemed to be getting closer to where more of the actual battling and massacre had taken place. I could feel the terror the spirits were trapped in. It was also starting to get late in the day and the sun was low in the sky. That also was contributing to the intensifying energy. I knew that there were many trapped souls there. If I focused on crossing one ghost at a time, the work could stretch on for hours and I didn't have hours. The only thing I could do was open up a big pillar of light and give as many spirits the opportunity to cross as I could. I focused on this, opening up the light and invoking the angels to help.

I did this for quite some time. I could feel many spirits crossing over. I could feel their relief as they crossed and let go of all the pain, terror, sadness, and loss they had been holding on to. I helped for as long as I could but then I felt how dark it was getting and I knew that we needed to start to make our way home. I had helped many spirits cross there but there were still others I did not have time to get to. There were many demons and dark entities around and I needed to ensure that my friends and I got home safely. As the light in the sky waned, the dark forces strengthened. I could also hear the sound of drums in the distance and it did not sound welcoming. It was definitely time to go.

We packed up our video equipment and started to make our way back to the car. The energy was getting more intense and it felt like the air was thick. By the time we made the trek all the way back to the parking lot and the car, the sun was already almost set. We quickly loaded everything into the car and tried to make our exit as quickly as possible. I could feel the demons and dark entities descending as we drove away. We wanted to get as much distance as possible from the massacre site before it was completely dark.

We were driving quickly, going 65 to 75 miles an hour, so it didn't take much time to put a bit of distance between us and the massacre site. I was starting to feel some relief as we got away from the intense and heavy energy that had started to descend on the site at nightfall. We were all exhausted. I checked in with my friends and Jan was tired but seemed to be doing alright. Alesa on the other hand was struggling. I asked her what was wrong and she said she was sad for those we hadn't had time to help. I understood this, of course I want to help as many as possible, but there seemed to be something else going on. I tuned in psychically to see what else was happening and was not surprised when I saw a trilobite entity on her heart. I worked with the angels to remove it and immediately felt her energy lighten. I heard her express a sigh of relief.

We chatted a little bit after that, but a short time later she fell asleep in the back seat. This kind of work can be exhausting. After an entity is attached and removed, the energy body (see terms for a description) has to heal and that takes a lot of energy too. Oftentimes, after something energetically taxing, our physical form needs extra rest, resources and healing too! There is something about this work that always makes me crave red meat. I don't eat meat all of the time but nothing will quite stabilize or ground and replenish me after a clearing like a hamburger or a steak. We did stop to eat and after that the rest of our journey was thankfully peaceful and uneventful.

Though I did as much as I could in a day, I know that there are still more to help at the Sand Creek massacre site. I hope to go back there some day to continue the work we started that day.

FOURTEEN
Spirits in the Light

Not all spirits are ghosts of course! Sometimes spirits who have crossed into the light will make an appearance here on the earth plane as well. They might come to visit loved ones or places that they enjoyed when they were alive or in body. They might be coming to support their loved ones, or just visit someone who is grieving their loss. There are many reasons for spirits in the light to come by for a visit. In fact, they come here a lot more often than most people realize! When I am communicating with a spirit on the other side for a client, they often show me that they spend a lot of time with their loved ones here. This sometimes surprises those who have been left behind as they may or may not feel the presence of the spirit.

As a general rule, the energy of a spirit in the light is more subtle than ghosts. For this reason, it took training and practice for me to learn how to see and sense them, whereas ghosts were often visible to me without any effort. Do not assume that because you haven't seen or sensed a loved one, that they are not visiting you. In addition to simply spending time with us and giving energetic support, they will often send us signs of their presence and love. Common signs include playing with electronics and turning lights on or off. Ghosts can do this too, but there is a usually a different energy with a spirit in the light. They might also send us an animal messenger. Some of the most common ones that spirits tell me they have sent to their loved ones are birds of all kinds, butterflies, dragonflies, and lady bugs. Nature is very connected with the spiritual realm, so sending an animal as a representative is quite common.

Other signs from a loved one can come in the form of references to their name, a song coming on the radio that makes you think of them, or in unusual cases, text messages or calls from them. If you think about your loved ones who have passed and there is nothing that has triggered their memory, this can be another way they are saying hello. The world of spirit works through telepathy or communicating via the mind so thinking about them can be a sign that they are actually saying hello!

Another common way for them to visit is through dreams. Our connection to the spiritual realm is naturally more open during sleep. We are more receptive and can hear their messages more directly. If you have had a very positive and vivid dream featuring your loved ones, it is very possible they have made you a visit during your dream time. This is nothing to fear! You can even ask for them to drop by.

While our loved ones often miss us, they do not usually have the same sense of loss as we do because they can see and sense us completely after they cross. It is almost like they are on the other side of a one way mirror. You see only the physical realm reflected back to you, but they can see us even though they are invisible to us. From the other side, they can also hear our thoughts and calls for help. If you are feeling lost and alone and want to reach out to loved ones on the other side, feel free to mentally ask them for help. You can also say the request out loud if that feels comfortable.

Spirit Guides

Our loved ones can act as spirit guides for us, giving us love and support and helping us on our path. They are not angels; generally angels and humans are different types of beings, though angelic souls can incarnate in human form. This is the exception however, so when we say that a loved one is our angel, it usually means they are acting like an angel and watching over us rather than that they are an actual angel.

We can also have spirit guides that we did not know in this life and perhaps even that we have not incarnated with. Sometimes these spirit guides can be quite vocal and reach out to us to communicate and help us. When some of my spirit guides started to reach out to me I was quite surprised since some of them are famous spirits and I was unclear why they would want to talk with me! As I have learned more about the spiritual realm, I have begun to understand that whether or not I think I know the spirits that have come to me, we are connected and it is best if I honor what they are communicating with me. I will share a couple of stories of spirits in the light and our communication. One main difference between communicating with a ghost and a spirit in the light is that spirits in the light have a greater perspective than ghosts do. Ghosts cannot see past their life circumstances and perspective and are often trapped in the limitations they had in life. These limitations can be physical limitations, beliefs, or mindsets. A spirit in the light on the other hand is literally a free spirit, can come and go at will, and is trying to assist us. Connecting with spirits in the light can be very helpful and illuminating whereas ghosts can often bring us down and may advise us based on their perceived limitations and perspective. I don't recommend following advice from ghosts for this reason.

The Icon

There are few spirits more famous than Marilyn Monroe. She touched the hearts and minds of people all over the world. I have always felt close to her and believe that she has been misunderstood. During one of my first trips to Hollywood as an adult, I decided to go on a Haunted Hollywood tour. This tour was advertised at the hotel where I was staying. My friend Jan was also travelling with me, so we contacted the tour agent and made the reservation. Once we got to the tour site, one of the things we learned was this was a new tour and they'd only just started it one month prior, in fact just in time for our visit!

We arrived for the start of the tour at the Chinese Theater and had several paranormal experiences including one at the theater itself. There was the spirit of an actor Victor Kilian who had been murdered nearby and is said to haunt the theater. The information I received from him was that the murder was not done by whom they thought it was. I also was attacked psychically by an angry spirit at the Hollywood Forever Cemetery. That particular spirit was not famous or infamous, just not at rest. It was a completely different experience at the

Roosevelt Hotel, however. We had learned that Marilyn Monroe had lived at the historic Roosevelt hotel on Hollywood Blvd. She had actually lived there for 2 years and it was the location of a photo shoot at the pool there that helped launch her into success.

The Haunted Hollywood tour did not actually take the participants to the Roosevelt hotel, so Jan and I decided to go to the hotel afterwards. We were having a drink at the beautiful pool bar when Marilyn Monroe showed up! She was definitely in the light. She had such beautiful and sweet energy. She showed me how she had been so young and hopeful in the beginning of her career. What I felt strongly was her idealism and hope. She was sad that she had lost a lot of that as she progressed in her career. It was such a beautiful moment! She came to me as she might have looked at her first photo shoot. She was in a bathing suit looking beautiful and more natural than she did in some later photos. I felt so blessed to have been touched by her presence.

FIFTEEN
The Stanley Hotel

I recently connected with a spirit in the light who surprised me! I had been getting the message to go to Estes Park from my angels and spirit guides and I had a women's weekend planned so I thought perhaps that was it. I asked for another sign and heard repeated references in the physical as well as psychically heard the word Stanley. A short time later, a friend of mine told me about the inaugural Stanley Horror Film Festival. I thought this was what the name Stanley was about so I asked for another sign and specifically wondered if the purpose of the festival involved films or ghosts and spirits. Shortly after asking, I turned on Pandora internet Radio and the song that came on was "Unchained Melody" by the Righteous Brothers from the movie *Ghost.* It was a confirmation of both actually since the song is in a movie about ghosts. Additionally, it is featured in a part of the movie that features Patrick Swayze's character trying to connect with someone after he has passed. After hearing this song, I knew it was a direct answer to my question. I decided to go to the festival.

The festival was wonderful and once I got there I was so glad I had come! The inaugural year featured the movie *The Shining* since the movie was inspired by the Stanley Hotel. Stephen King wrote a good part of the book at the hotel and used the hotel as inspiration for the story. Because of the importance of the movie and the relevance in the horror genre, there was quite a bit on the movie at the first festival. They showed the movie on the lawn of the hotel at night and one of the featured films was the movie *Room 237* about the making of *The Shining* and hidden messages that the director, Stanley Kubrick, may have placed in the movie.

Room 237 featured interviews by various experts who had studied the film and had ideas about what the secret meaning of the film was. Stanley Kubrick was a very cryptic fellow and so it is difficult to know what he really intended. He did not answer questions about the meaning of his films very directly and on top of that, he died in 1999. After the screening of that particular film, several of the experts from the film were onsite and one of the recurring statements was, "we can't ask Stanley Kubrick." Of course they meant because he is no longer in the earthly realm. While I recognized that, I was not sure if that was actually true for me since that is one of the things I specialize in: talking with those on the other side!

The next day they had a panel of experts on *The Shining* including Mick Garris, director of *The Shining* TV Mini-Series; Leon Vitali, assistant to Stanley Kubrick for *The Shining* (the movie); and the director of the documentary *Room 237,* Rodney Ascher. Once again the topic of Stanley Kubrick came up. After the panel I thought why not see if I could connect with Stanley?

My friend and videographer, Jan, had come with me, so we got some lunch and then set up our equipment. I opened up the channel, and boy was I surprised!

Stanley was there alright and ready to talk with me. Not only that, he indicated he'd been waiting for me! Suddenly the references to the name Stanley had new meaning. Not just the Stanley hotel and film fest but Stanley Kubrick himself! I was blown away. I asked him what he wanted to communicate. He had some personal messages for me and some general statements as well. One of the things that amazed me was that he showed me that inside my heart was a film reel. Basically that in my heart was film! This completely made sense as I have always been completely fascinated and drawn to film. I studied theater in college, not for the love of theater (though I do love it) but primarily because the university I was attending did not have a film acting program, only theater acting.

Stanley also showed me several cryptic things including a very clear visual of a small fish getting eaten by a bigger fish, which then got eaten by an even bigger fish, and so on and so forth. Then he said, "There is always a bigger fish!" Of course this has many potential meanings in life and on the other side. The whole conversation with Stanley was very enlightening and showed me that I should never assume who might want to talk with me from the other side! Stanley also showed me how he had helped with the festival itself - he'd helped orchestrate it from the other side. When I learned this it made a lot of sense because the festival had come together very quickly and came off very well – particularly since they had a short amount of time to organize it. There was great attendance and many participants from Los Angeles and from even farther away. It was not bad for a first time effort.

I believe he had a hand in the following year as well. Once again the festival was put together on short notice. Up until 1 month beforehand, the festival website still had last year's schedule listed on it. Then a few weeks beforehand, I was asked to hold a séance as part of their immersion game for participants. I was very happy to participate professionally and once again Stanley Kubrick showed up, this time for the séance. Stanley is a great example of a spirit in the light who is still doing work from the other side. Since he worked through the medium of film in life, it completely makes sense that he would work through the medium of film from the after-life as well! Those on the other side oftentimes don't simply stop what they are doing but they find a way to continue their work from there. In many cases, they need live people to partner with and it helps if those people can sense and communicate with them. One more reason why I encourage everyone to tap into their own psychic gifts – you just never know who you might end up talking to.

SIXTEEN
Connecting with Spirits

If you'd like to communicate with spirits in the light there are many ways to do this. I don't recommend communicating with ghosts, or participating in ghost hunting unless you have training. With paranormal work, I think it is worth asking: who is hunting who? I have known many amateur paranormal investigators who have brought home unhappy and destructive ghosts or even demons and had unpleasant consequences as a result. If you don't have spiritual tools and protections, this can be hazardous work. For those wanting to learn more about how to communicate with and assist ghosts in crossing over, I do teach classes on the subject. Feel free to look at my website to see my current class offerings on the topic: www.healingpowers.net.

If you want to connect with spirits in the light, there are many ways to do this that can be fun, comforting and helpful. Connecting with and receiving communications with a loved one on the other side can provide closure and emotional release. Sometimes they can give us guidance, but do keep in mind their soul remains the same. If someone struggled in a specific area in life, they may not be the best person to ask about the topic in death. For example, someone who had several unhappy marriages is still working on love karma-wise so it might be best to ask for advice from them on other topics.

Ouija Boards

For a highly trained psychic, Ouija boards can be an effective communication tool. For most people however, it is likely to create a door or opening to beings that may or may not have your interest at heart. Prior to attempting to communicate with spirits, it is imperative to invoke protection and clear any energies that aren't loving. Since most people do not know how to do this properly, using a Ouija board can be like playing with fire. I am definitely not an advocate of using a Ouija board with children. I actually think it is highly irresponsible to sell it as a children's game. If you have or use one of these, be very cautious and stop the communication immediately if anything dark starts to come through. Also ask the angels to remove any unloving beings or energies from you or your space.

Hiring a Professional

Hiring a professional psychic medium can be an incredible experience! It is important to hire someone reputable and trustworthy. As in any field, there are those who are either not legitimate or are manipulative. If something feels "off", it probably is, so trust your intuition when hiring someone. You might find it helpful to ask how they work before you hire them. That is not the same thing as asking a medium questions about your loved one, if they are there, and what they have to say prior to a reading. If you do that, essentially you are asking the medium to do a reading prior to the reading! I also find it helpful to know prior to opening up the channel if there is someone in particular you'd like to communicate with since there are often so many spirits wanting to talk with us. Without guidance, I may not automatically start to speak with the spirit you'd most want to talk to. For example if your Aunt Barbara was loud and pushy, but you want to talk to your mom Rose, do not be surprised if Barbara is the one who steps forward first! Spirits' personality traits usually remain very similar to how they were in life.

If you go to a medium, you might find it helpful to bring a list of questions for the spirit, or you can simply see what they want to communicate with you. Do not be surprised if their priorities have shifted since they were here. Old grudges may disappear or they simply may no longer care about the earthly concerns they were wrapped up in. For example, they may care very little about money, even if they were money-focused in their life, and instead encourage you to focus on your happiness and relationships.

Keep in mind different mediums work in different ways. Some are clairvoyant (seers), some are clairaudient (they hear spirits), and others are empathic or receive information through touching an object that belonged to the person. None of these is better or worse than other gifts, but I recommend finding out how the psychic works so that you can be prepared and better understand that psychic's process.

I sometimes come across clients who want proof that the process is real or that the person being communicated with is the loved one they want to connect with. This is completely understandable, however, I want people to know that skepticism or closed energy on the part of the client can block or inhibit the process. Usually something is communicated that shows the client the spirit is the one they want to talk with however this is not always the case. Some spirits have no interest in proving anything or the signs are confusing and hard to interpret as a reader. I recommend keeping an open mind and asking questions while also being open to what the spirit wants to communicate.

Holding a Séance

Since most readings with mediums are done with just one or maybe a few people, holding a séance can be a great way to connect with loved ones and spirits for larger groups. In a séance, the reader invokes the spirits, and acts as a channel, relaying information that comes through. Usually the spirits that are channeled are somehow connected with the séance participants though it is possible for a wandering spirit or ghost to drop in simply to say hello or to ask for help. While these are often depicted as spooky events in movies, they can be quite light and healing experiences as well. Again, it is important to find a professional that is competent, uses psychic protection tools, and has integrity.

Ghost Hunts

As I mentioned before, going on a ghost hunt or doing paranormal work is something to be taken seriously! Many people think of this as a game, but this realm and world are very serious. Find a reputable group to work with and I highly encourage anyone going on a paranormal investigation or ghost tour to ask the angels for protection in advance. I also recommend asking the angels for assistance with clearing any unloving energy or beings afterwards. Do this also if you are going to a place that is reputed to be haunted, whether or not your visit has anything to do with the paranormal.

Communicating with Spirits

There are many ways for you to receive direct communication with spirits. You can learn psychic development tools and learn what your psychic gifts are and then communicate with them directly. There are many people who have psychic gifts that are completely unaware of them. My mother is a perfect example. When I started taking psychic classes and learning how to open up my own psychic abilities, I would tell her about some of the things I was learning and experiencing. Often times she would get a funny look on her face and then I would say, "does that happen to you?" and she'd say yes! My mom is very psychic but never knew it because she simply didn't know much about how it all worked. I am guessing this is the case for many of you who are reading this now.

If you have seen or sensed ghosts that means you do have some psychic abilities. Even if you haven't sensed them, you likely still do have psychic abilities! I believe everyone has some psychic abilities but some people's abilities are a lot stronger than others. For example, most people can paint or draw something; some might be able to draw a stick figure, while others can create masterpieces. It is important to honor your natural gifts but also understand that some of them might need to be developed to come to their full potential. Even the masters study. It is very rare for someone's gifts to be so strong that they don't need some training and development.

Asking for Signs

It can be very effective to ask your loved ones to send you a message. They might send a dream to you or someone you know. They can cause a song to play that makes you think of them. Or something might come up in conversation that makes you think of them. They can also send you physical signs such as finding coins or pennies repeatedly or in unusual places. They might also create rainbows or images in clouds for you to see. You can ask for a general sign or a specific sign, but consider that specific signs might take longer for them to coordinate, so if you ask for a specific sign, have patience.

Bear in mind that our loved ones on the other side want to communicate with us, but it isn't always easy for us to receive their messages. They are on a different plane of existence than our physical bodies. Imagine energy as broadcasting channels. When our body dies, the radio channel changes to a different frequency. Through psychic training or by going to a medium, you can learn to tune into or connect with these other frequencies. It is easier to communicate with ghosts because they are still on our channel in the physical plane, but imagine it is like the power went out and they don't have a microphone anymore! In fact EVPs (electronic voice phenomenon) are usually much quieter than live human voices. Oftentimes the recordings are only audible once the volume level is raised dramatically above human hearing levels.

SEVENTEEN
Clearing Spaces

Much of this work is intentional. You do not have to be a psychic like me to help spirits cross over and clear spaces. Consider that a lot of people have latent psychic talents they are not aware of. So many are like my mother, unaware of their psychic gifts until they receive training. If you are drawn to this work, it is very likely you have some untapped abilities. In fact, everyone has some level of psychic ability, and the natural inclination varies from individual to individual just like anyone else.

The tips I give here are for spirits that are easy going and not aggressive. If you are dealing with a very nasty, angry and powerful ghost, a poltergeist, or a demon or powerful dark entity, I do recommend bringing in a professional. Signs that the spirit or dark entity/demon qualifies for professional assistance can include one or more of the following:

- Objects in your home breaking

- Major and recurring plumbing problems
- Foul smells you can't explain
- A cockroach or fly problem
- People or animals becoming seriously ill or dying
- Extreme dissension or problems in relationships
- Intense or very scary dreams or nightmares
- Inability to sleep
- Night paralysis or feeling like you are being suffocated or held down while you sleep
- Seeing or sensing spirits that are acting angry and territorial in your space
- Unexplained injuries or bruises, cuts or scratches

If one of more of these signs is present in your home or business, I do recommend hiring a professional. I also recommend hiring a professional if satanic or other very dark rituals invoking demons or dark entities were done in or around your space. A note about witchcraft: there is dark and light witchcraft, however I have noted with some of my clients who are practicing witchcraft that they are not always clearly able to discern the light magic from the dark magic. So I recommend practicing it with caution. There are many spirits and entities that will create the illusion of working for the light while actually being quite dark. If you decide to go the route of hiring a professional, use your intuition about whom to hire. If you get a bad feeling from that individual, honor that, even if they are an expert. Trust yourself and your own intuition. I do sometimes travel to client's homes for blessings and clearings and there are many I have trained who are also qualified to do this work.

With all that said, if you have a spirit that is in your space or you are feeling some kind of presence, there are things you can do on your own. I also do live trainings and teleclasses for this work if you feel you have some psychic ability and would like to learn more about how to handle these situations for yourself.

Tools of the Trade

Prior to doing this work, there are some items that can be helpful. They are not required to do this work as the angels are the most powerful resource of all, however I do recommend having one or more of these items on hand. I'll list them first and then go into detail on how to use each one and why they are useful.

- **Sage**
- **Palo Santo**
- **Cedar**
- **Sage Spray**
- **White candles**
- **Wood Matches**
- **Cleaning Supplies**
- **Holy Water**

Sage is a plant that was used by Native Americans for its clearing and purifying properties. This is different variety of sage than garden sage which is used for cooking and is considered an herb. The sage plant grows as a bush and is native to North America. It is harvested and bundled with string and then dried. Once it is dried and bundled, it is called a smudge stick. It can then be burned and the smoke itself helps to clear stagnant and negative energy. Simply use matches to light the tip of the bundle and then waft the smoke over the space you'd like to clear. Be sure to get into any areas that don't get a lot of air flow like closets, cupboards, under the bed, etc. You can use this method to clear yourself of negative energy as well. Be sure to use a fire safe plate or some other object to catch the ashes. I often use a cookie pan when I am clearing a large space. Bundles come in various sizes; the smaller ones are usually good for travelling or clearing yourself. For an entire home or larger spaces, I usually get a large bundle that is 8 or 9 inches long because it smokes better and is more efficient.

There are many different types of sage such as desert sage, purple sage, and white sage. I like using white sage as I find it to be very strong and effective. You might also find that there is sage growing naturally in your area. There is a lot of desert sage in Colorado and white sage in California so you might even try to harvest some yourself. Since this plant tends to grow in very dry climates, if you are trying to grow some yourself, be very careful about overwatering. The smoke from the sage plant is very strong and depending on the variety and the age of the plant at harvest can either smell sweet or acrid.

Palo Santo's name literally means holy wood. It grows naturally in South America and is related to frankincense, myrrh, and copal. It has a very sweet smelling smoke and brings in a very high vibrational energy to the space in which it is burned. You can usually find palo santo cut into small pieces which you light and let smoke. I recommend using after sage to bring in a light, positive energy into your space, or you can use it much like incense and just let the scent fill up the room. Palo santo has been used by humans for its healing and uplifting properties for millennia. In fact the Incas used it to purify the spirit. Not only can it be burned but you can also drink palo santo tea and use it in other beneficial ways for the body.

Cedar can be used much like palo santo. It has very uplifting properties. You can use it to lighten the energy and to purify a space. Cedar is an evergreen tree with a very pure energy. It is not a coincidence that cedar is used to keep stored clothing or shoes fresh. Cedar essential oil is also lovely and has many wonderful properties. Cedar is usually sold in bundles, much like sage, though you can also purchase loose cedar needles and sage leaves to burn in a sacred fire.

Sage spray has a liquid base with essences of sage and sometimes essential oils or crystal essences. It usually comes in a spray bottle and can also be helpful to use for clearing spaces or freshening up the energy. I use it on myself regularly when I feel I've absorbed negative energy. It is great for travelling or in circumstances in which it is unsafe or prohibited to burn or smoke anything such as on a plane or hotel room. I like *Smudge in Spray* by The Crystal Garden for its energy qualities and refreshing scent. In my experience you cannot overuse this stuff, but you will likely feel the energy shift once you've used it.

White candles are great to use for ghosts in particular. You can light the white candle and help create light for a spirit to cross. Just as with anything involving fire, please use a fire safe container and do not leave any flames unattended.

Holy water can also be helpful to use to help bless a space or remove negative energy or intentions. Holy water is blessed water, however it often also has salt added which has additional clearing properties. You can use the holy water on doors or walls; you can also brush holy water over surfaces that were used in dark ritual magic. For example if there was a floor or wall on which satanic marks were painted or drawn, the holy water can help clear those negative intentions. Not all holy waters are created equally of course. I like to use blessed water from the city of Lourdes in France.

Clearing and Blessing Process

Of course, there are many ways to clear and bless a space. Here is a simple one you can do. Again for very dark energy or aggressive ghosts, calling in a specialist is recommended.

Invoke the Archangels – I recommend calling in Archangels Michael, Raphael, Chamuel, Jophiel and Azrael. Calling in other angels and spirit guides is always beneficial also. You can also invite Jesus, Buddha, Mohammed, or any spiritual figure that you feel connected to, to assist in the process. Specifically ask them to protect you and the space, assist in the process, and help you with any specific guidance that would help in your particular situation.

Ask the angels to clear any beings or energies that are not of the light and take them permanently away. The permanently part is very important as without that specific statement, they may be allowed to return. Do not rush this part. You may need to move room to room or even deal with smaller areas one at a time. For example, if a particular closet feels dark or your child dislikes a particular room, you may want to spend extra time in those spaces. Move along only when you feel the energy shift. Visualize light coming in and flooding the area with light and the angels escorting any beings that are not of the light away.

If you feel there are earthbound spirits, ask the angels to open the light and help them cross. You can light a white candle and set the intention that the light will help guide the spirit. Visualize a pillar of light or a stairway going from the material plane into the after-life. Loved ones from the other side or angels may appear to help the spirit cross. Ask the angels to close the light portal once the spirit has crossed so you don't draw in other beings that are in the surrounding areas into your space.

Ask the angels to clear any energy that has been released with the crossing of the spirits and take it into the light. This is quite common when spirits cross. I will feel so positive and hopeful because I am feeling what the spirit felt and then all of a sudden the space will feel heavy. Once the angels have cleared away any energy residues or debris that was released, the space will feel much lighter again!

After the previous steps have been done, burn sage to clear the space of any stubborn energy residue. Don't hurry this part either, and, as I mentioned before, make sure to get into the corners of rooms, under beds, etc. Open the windows to help the smoke clear out of the room as well. I recommend doing this in each room after you have done the previous two steps.

If you have some on hand, I recommend following the sage with palo santo or cedar to bring in light energy. This is not required, but just brings in that light energy. Just as with the sage, use a fire safe container for the ashes. You can also follow this with the spray smudge or just skip the regular sage and go right to the spray smudge after the clearing work with the angels if your circumstances prohibit burning anything.

Finally, ask the angels to continue to protect you and the space. I suggest stationing angels on all sides of your home including above and below. You can also ask the angels to surround your space with white light so that if any spirit tries to come in it will automatically be crossed. Since the light is a gateway or portal to the other side, a spirit will then cross if it goes into this light.

These above steps are only an overview of how to do a space clearing. I am also working on a more thorough guide for those that do this work. Expect it sometime in the next couple of years so stay tuned for that book as well.

This work is complex but very rewarding. Many blessings to you on your journey in this wild, and often unknown world of spirit. Know that you are truly never alone and the angels are always here to help you! Remember that the light is always stronger than the dark and the fear of the unknown is usually more frightening than the unknown itself.

Afterword

I want everyone to know that while not everyone may have the same gifts that I have, we all have ways of connecting and receiving information. Most of us are far more intuitive than we give ourselves credit for. I encourage everyone reading this book to start tuning in and learning more about what their own gifts are. The world will be a much easier place if we are all using and connecting with each other through the gifts that we were given. I wish each of you the best on your own journey and invite you to ask your spirit guides and angels to help you along the way.

There is a lot of fear regarding the spiritual and unseen worlds. I encourage everyone reading this to explore in a safe way. Ask the angels for guidance and support on your journey and through your exploration. When I opened this door for myself, the results were nothing short of incredible. Of course it is important to connect with and receive guidance from the light spirits only. Asking dark entities, demons, or angry ghosts for help is only going to result with you on the losing end of the bargain. Angels, on the other hand, are only here to help us. If you want more information on how to work with the angelic realm, you can read my book *Angels: How to Understand, Recognize, and Receive Their Guidance*. The most important thing to remember when dealing with darker beings is that fear is what they feed on. If you do not nourish them, they will usually leave. Fear holds us back and keeps us from experiencing light and love.

I am sending love and light to you and hope you can move forward on your illuminated path with a better understanding of the spiritual realm.

With love,
Laura Powers

Helpful Terms

Angel Communicator – Someone who can communicate through one or more senses (sight, hearing, feeling) with angels.

Clairalience – Clear smelling or receiving information from your sense of smell; also called clairescence. This is a form of extra sensory perception or ESP.

Clairaudient – Clear hearing or hearing sounds that are not just on the physical plane. This can be hearing a sound with your ears or hearing the word or phrase in your mind like a thought which isn't yours. This is a form of extra sensory perception or ESP.

Claircognizance – Clear knowing or knowing something you have no logical way of knowing. This is a form of extra sensory perception or ESP.

Clairgustance – The ability to taste something that you have not put in your mouth. This is a form of extra sensory perception or ESP.

Clairsentience – Clear feeling or feeling something that is coming from outside of you. This can be a physical sensation or emotion. This is a form of extra sensory perception or ESP.

Clairvoyance – Clear seeing or seeing something that is not on the physical plane. Clairvoyance can be experienced with your physical eyes or with your third or internal eye. This is a form of Extra Sensory Perception or ESP.

Cord – An energetic connection between people, places, and things which transmits energy and emotions.

Demon – A supernatural energy being that feeds on and creates darkness in the world. Often used within the context of religion.

Devil – A dark and malevolent leader of hell and demons. Usually used within a Judeo-Christian context.

Empathy – The ability to feel what others are feeling. A form of Extra Sensory Perception or ESP.

Energy body – The energetic part of our body; we are made of matter and energy, and both parts come together to form us.

Entity – An energetic being that does not have a physical form. Entities are non-human and they are not animals or angels either but some other type of being. There are many different types of entities.

EVPs (Electronic Voice Phenomenon) – Electronic recordings that are believed to have been caused by paranormal activity.

Extra Sensory Perception (ESP) – One or more heightened senses that perceive more than the normal range of sensing.

Ghosts – An earth bound spirit or the spirit of a person whose body had died and whose soul or spirit has not crossed into the light.

Medium – Someone who can communicate with ghosts (earth bound spirits) and spirits (people without a body that are not earth bound).

Near-death experience (NDE) – A personal experience, in which a person experiences the continuation of their consciousness even after the clinical death of their body.

Out-of-body experience (OBE) – A phenomenon in which an individual experiences their soul separating from their body. Usually the individual will then witness their body separately from them. The soul can then travel freely without the physical limitations of the body.

Paranormal – events that are outside the realm of normal experience and cannot be explained by current science.

Parapsychology – A term coined in 1889 to describe research of the paranormal. Max Dessoir created the term by combining the words for "para" which means alongside, with the word psychology. The clair-senses, precognition, telepathy, psychokinesis, ghosts and other paranormal experiences are scientifically studied in parapsychology.

Precognition – Knowing something is going to happen before it does with no logical way of knowing this. A form of Extra Sensory Perception or ESP.

Psychokinesis - The ability to move matter with your mind.

Psychometry – The ability to receive information from an object through touch.

Remote Viewing – A psychic exercise in which a location is viewed from a remote location using clairvoyance or psychic sight.

Sage – A plant that can be used to clear negative or stagnant energy.

Shaman – A person who is trained to communicate and work with the spirit realm. Shamans are found in indigenous cultures throughout the world.

Spirit – The non-physical manifestation of a person or being. The spirit never dies and is made of energy.

Telepathy – The ability to communicate with others through thoughts.

Sources

These are books and websites that I referenced for this book and that have informed me and my work:

303 Cycling. *Erie Velodrome Takes On Damage After Storm.* 2014. http://303cycling.com/erie-velodrome-takes-on-damage-after-storm

About.com. *All About EVP.* 2014. http://paranormal.about.com/od/ghostaudiovideo/a/All-About-EVP.htm

Allen, Sue. *Spirit Release*. John Hunt Publishing. 2010.

Backman, Linda. *Bringing Your Soul to Light*. Llewellyn Worldwide Ltd., 2009.

Belanger, Michelle. *Dictionary of Demons: Names of the Damned.* Llewellyn Publications, 2010.

Belanger, Michelle. *Haunting Experiences: Encounters with the Otherworldly.* Llewellyn Publications, 2009.

Belanger, Michelle. *Psychic Vampire Codex: A Manual of Magick and Energy Work*. Red Wheel/Weiser, LLC, 2004.

Belanger, Michelle. *The Ghost Hunter's Survival Guide: Personal Protection Techniques for Encounters with the Paranormal.* Llewellyn Publications, 2009.

Blog. Nola. *Old State Capitol Still Occupied by Former Ghosts.* 2014.

http://blog.nola.com/SELU/2009/10/old_state_capitol_still_occupi.html

Burney, Diane. *Spiritual Clearings: Sacred Practices to Release Negative Energy and Harmonize Your Life*. North Atlantic Books, 2010.

Byrne, Rhonda. *The Secret*. Atria Books, 2006.

Briggs, Constance Victoria. *Encyclopedia of the Unseen World: The Ultimate Guide to Apparitions, Death Bed Visions, Mediums, Shadow People, Wandering Spirits, and Much, Much More*. Red Wheel/Weiser, 2010.

Cheesman Park. *Facts About Cheesman Park*. 2014. http://cheesmanpark.net/01/pages/facts-01.html

Choquette, Sonia. *Ask Your Guides*. Hay House Inc., 2007.

Colorado Hometown Weekly. *Velodrome Asks Help*. 2014. http://www.coloradohometownweekly.com/news/erie/ci_26816306/velodrome-asks-help

Constantine. Dir. Francis Lawrence. Perf. Keanu Reeves, Rachel Weisz, Shia LaBeouf, and Tilda Swinton. Warner Bros. Pictures, 2005. Film.

Daily Camera. *Crews Work Rebuild Boulder Valley Velodrome After Erie*. 2014. http://www.dailycamera.com/erie-news/ci_23813225/crews-work-rebuild-boulder-valley-velodrome-after-erie

Four Seasons Productions. (2007-2011). *Paranormal State* [Television Series]. Pennsylvania, PA: Arts & Entertainment Network.

Ghost. Dir. Jerry Zucker. Perf. Patrick Swayze, Demi Moore, Whoopi Goldberg, and Tony Goldwyn. Paramount Pictures, 1990. Film.

Ghost Busters. Dir. Ivan Reitman. Perf. Bill Murray, Dan Aykroyd, Sigourney Weaver, and Harold Ramis. Columbia Pictures, 1984. Film.

Ghost Town. Dir. David Koepp. Perf. Ricky Gervais, Greg Kinnear, and Tea Leoni. Dreamworks, 2008. Film.

Google. *Poltergeist.* 2014. https://www.google.com/#q=poltergeist

Greer, John Michael. *The New Encyclopedia of the Occult.* Llewellyn Publications, 2003.

Guiley, Rosemary Ellen. *The Encyclopedia of Demons and Demonology.*

Insidious: Chapter 2. Dir. James Wan. Perf. Patrick Wilson, Rose Bryne, and Barbara

Hershey. FilmDistrict, 2013. Film.

Kubrick, Stanley (1928-1999) was a film director with famous titles like *Eyes Wide Shut, Full Metal Jacket, The Shining,* and *A Clockwork Orange*.

Mercer Online. *Seven Fires Council: Our People, Our Future.* 2014. http://www.merceronline.com/Native/native10.htm

Moss, Nan. *Weather Shamanism: Harmonizing Our Connection with the Elements.* Bear & Company, 2008.

Murphey, Cecil and Piper, Don. *90 Minutes in Heaven: A True Story of Life and Death.* Revell, 2007.

National Park Service. *The Sand Creek Massacre – 8 Hours that changed the Great Plains forever*. 2014. http://www.nps.gov/sand/index.htm

National Park Service. *Sand Creek Massacre National Historic Site*. 2014. http://www.nps.gov/nr/travel/cultural_diversity/Sand_Creek_Massacre_National_Historic_Site.html

Newton, Michael. *Journey of Souls: Case Studies of Life Between Lives*. Llewellyn Worldwide Ltd., 1996.

Peter Pan. Dir. Clyde Geronimi, Wilfred Jackson, and Hamilton Luske. Perf. Bobby Driscoll, Kathryn Beaumont, Hans Conried, and Paul Collins. Walt Disney Productions, 1953. Film.

Picturemaker Productions. (2005-2011). *Medium* [Television Series]. Los Angeles, CA: NBC.

Prairie Ghosts. *Hollywood's Haunted Movie Theaters.* 2014. http://www.prairieghosts.com/hollywood12.html

Prince, Derek. *They Shall Expel Demons*. Amazon Digital Services, 1998.

Room 237. Dir. Rodney Asher. Perf. Bill Blakemore, Geoffrey Cocks, and Juli Kearns. Highland Park Classics, 2012. Film.

Sand Creek Site. *Sand Creek Massacre National Historic Site.* 2014. http://www.sandcreeksite.com/

Sanders/Moses Productions. (2005-2010). *Ghost Whisperer* [Television Series]. Los Angeles, CA: CBS.

Schwartz, Robert. *Your Soul's Plan: Discovering the Real Meaning of The Life You Planned Before You Were Born.* North Atlantic Books. 2010.

Seeing Stars in Hollywood. *The Roosevelt Hotel.* 2014. http://www.seeing-stars.com/Hotels/HollywoodRoosevelt.shtml

The Dead. Dir. John Huston. Perf. Anjelica Huston, Donal McCann, Dan O'Herlihy, and Donal Donnelly. Vestron Pictures, 1987. Film.

The Killing Room. Dir. Jonathan Liebesman. Perf. Chloe Sevigny, Nick Cannon, Timothy Hutton, and Clea DuVall. ContentFilm, 2009. Film.

The Others. Dir. Alejandro Amenabar. Perf. Nicole Kidman, Fionnula Flanagan, Christopher Eccleston, and Elaine Cassidy. Miramax Films, 2001. Film.

The Wizard of Oz. Dir. Victor Fleming. Perf. Judy Garland, Frank Morgan, Ray Bolger, and Bert Lahr. Metro-Goldwyn-Mayer, 1939. Film.

Vitali, Leon (1948-) is a well-known actor who starred in famous titles, such as *Eyes Wide Shut, Terror of Frankenstein*, and *Inter Rail.*

Virtue, Doreen. *Earth Angels.* Hay House, 2002.

Wikipedia. Arapaho. 2015. http://en.wikipedia.org/wiki/Arapaho

Wikipedia. *Black Kettle.* 2014. http://en.wikipedia.org/wiki/Black_Kettle

Wikipedia. *Colorado.* 2014. http://en.wikipedia.org/wiki/Colorado

Wikipedia. *Devil.* 2014. http://en.wikipedia.org/wiki/Devil

Wikipedia. *Electronic Voice Phenomenon*. 2014 http://en.wikipedia.org/wiki/Electronic_voice_phenomenon

Wikipedia. *John Evans*. 2014. http://en.wikipedia.org/wiki/John_Evans_(governor)

Wikipedia. *Louisina State Capitol*. 2014. http://en.wikipedia.org/wiki/Louisiana_State_Capitol

Wikipedia. *Paranormal*. 2014. http://en.wikipedia.org/wiki/Paranormal

Wikipedia. *Room 237*. 2014. http://en.wikipedia.org/wiki/Room_237

Wikipedia. Salvia. 2015. http://en.wikipedia.org/wiki/Salvia_officinalis

Wikipedia. Salvia apiana. 2015. http://en.wikipedia.org/wiki/Salvia_apiana

Wikipedia. *Sand Creek Massacre National Historic Site*. 2014. http://en.wikipedia.org/wiki/Sand_Creek_Massacre_National_Historic_Site

Wikipedia. Smudge Stick. 2015.
http://en.wikipedia.org/wiki/Smudge_stick

Wikipedia. *The Roosevelt Hotel.* 2014.
http://en.wikipedia.org/wiki/Hollywood_Roosevelt_Hotel

Media Related to Work in This Field

Afterlife, produced and directed by Paul Perry, examines the topic of the afterlife through examining near-death experiences and research: http://www.imdb.com/title/tt3408818/

Celebrity Ghost Stories is a television series that features interviews with celebrities about their experiences with ghosts and paranormal events. http://www.imdb.com/title/tt1320080/

Constantine, directed by Francis Lawrence, is a supernatural thriller that tells the story of irreverent supernatural detective John Constantine, who has literally been to hell and back. http://www.imdb.com/title/tt0360486/

Crossing Over with John Edward is a television series that features John Edward, a psychic that communicates with his audience's dead relatives. http://www.imdb.com/title/tt0292776/

Defending Your Life is a film directed by Albert Books that shows people trying to prove their courage in the afterlife. http://www.imdb.com/title/tt0101698/

Ghost, directed by Jerry Zucker, is a film about a man whose love for his partner lets him remain on earth as a ghost after he dies. http://www.imdb.com/title/tt0099653/

Ghost Adventures is a television series that features Zak Bagans, Nick Groff, and Aaron Goodwin investigating the scariest and most haunted places in the world. http://www.imdb.com/title/tt1319900/

Ghost Hunters is a television series that features a group of real paranormal researchers investigating many haunted houses around the country. http://www.imdb.com/title/tt0426697/

Ghost Town, directed by David Koepp, is about a man who dies, but is revived seven minutes later and then has the ability to see ghosts who then annoy him. http://www.imdb.com/title/tt0995039/

Ghost Whisperer, directed by John Gray, is about a woman who has the ability to speak to spirits of the recently deceased and tries to help them send their messages so they can pass to the other side. http://www.imdb.com/title/tt0460644/

Haunted Hotels is a television series that features haunted hotels from the US, UK, and France. http://www.imdb.com/title/tt0379629/

Insidious, directed by James Wan, is about a family that tries to stop evil spirits from trapping their comatose child in a realm called The Further. http://www.imdb.com/title/tt1591095/

Insidious: Chapter 2, directed by Jan Wan, is about a family that seeks to uncover the mysterious childhood secret that has left them dangerously connected to the spirit world. http://www.imdb.com/title/tt2226417

Jacob's Ladder, directed by Adrian Lyne, is about a haunted Vietnam war veteran that tries to discover his past while suffering from a severe case of dissociation. http://www.imdb.com/title/tt0099871/

Long Island Medium is a television series that follows psychic and medium Theresa Caputo, going to random people and communicating with their deceased loved ones . http://www.imdb.com/title/tt2010806/

Medium is a television series about a suburban mom who attempts to balance her family life and also solve mysteries. She has a gift that makes her see visions of death and crimes in her sleep. http://www.imdb.com/title/tt0412175/

Odd Thomas, directed by Stephen Sommers, is about a short-order cook with clairvoyant abilities who encounters a man with a link to dark, threatening forces. http://www.imdb.com/title/tt1767354/

Paranormal Witness is a television series that recreates stories of people who have lived through paranormal experiences. http://www.imdb.com/title/tt1874066/

Poltergeist, directed by Tobe Hooper, is about a family's home that is haunted by a host of ghosts. http://www.imdb.com/title/tt0084516/

Psychic Kids: Children of the Paranormal is a television series that features Dr. Lisa Miller helping psychic children deal with their powers and understanding their abilities. http://www.imdb.com/title/tt1300017/

Red Lights, directed by Rodrigo Cortes, is about a psychologist who studies paranormal activity. He begins to investigate a famous psychic who resurfaces after the psychic's toughest critic mysteriously dies. http://www.imdb.com/title/tt1748179/

Supernatural is a television series about two brothers fighting evil supernatural beings. http://www.imdb.com/title/tt0460681/

The After Life Investigations is a documentary about four afterlife investigations that present scientific evidence that the paranormal phenomenon being investigated were indeed real. http://www.theafterlifeinvestigations.com/#!synopsis

The Awakening, directed by Nick Murphy, is about a hoax exposer who visits a haunted boarding school to explain sightings of a child ghost. http://www.imdb.com/title/tt1687901/

The Conjuring, directed by James Wan, is about paranormal investigators who work to help a family terrorized by a dark presence in their farmhouse. http://www.imdb.com/title/tt1457767/

The Dead Files, is a television series about a retired homicide detective that is paired up with a psychic communicator to explore supernatural cases. http://www.imdb.com/title/tt2012511/

The Exorcist, directed by William Friedkin, is about a teenage girl who is possessed by a mysterious entity. Her mother seeks the help of two priests to save her daughter. http://www.imdb.com/title/tt0070047/

The Fly, directed by David Cronenberg, is about a brilliant but eccentric scientist who begins to transform into a giant man/fly hybrid after one of his experiments goes horribly wrong. http://www.imdb.com/title/tt0091064/

The Haunted is a television series that features true stories about animals, their owners and their supernatural experiences. http://www.imdb.com/title/tt1566020/

The Haunting, directed by Jan de Bont, is about three people who take part in a sleep study in a huge mansion that happens to be haunted. http://www.imdb.com/title/tt0171363/

The Others, directed by Alejandro Amenabar, is about a woman who lives in a darkened old house with her photosensitive children and becomes convinced that her home is haunted. http://www.imdb.com/title/tt0230600/

The Rite, directed by Mikael Hafstrom, is about an American seminary student who travels to Italy to take an exorcism course. http://www.imdb.com/title/tt1161864/

The Sixth Sense, directed by M. Night Shyamalan, is about a boy who communicates with spirits who don't know they are dead who then seeks the help of a child psychologist. http://www.imdb.com/title/tt0167404/

Stay tuned for Laura's forthcoming books about manifesting and *Diary of a Ghost Whisperer: Gulf Coast Edition*!

For additional information, go to www.healingpowers.net. To receive updates about Laura's books, speaking engagements, events, TV show and more, submit your info on the subscribe page.

Notes

Notes

Notes

Made in the USA
San Bernardino, CA
03 May 2015